**New Directions for
Teaching and Learning**

Catherine M. Wehlburg
EDITOR-IN-CHIEF

Faculty and First-Generation College Students:
Bridging the Classroom Gap Together

Vickie L. Harvey
Teresa Heinz Housel
EDITORS

Number 127 • Fall 2011
Jossey-Bass
San Francisco

FACULTY AND FIRST-GENERATION COLLEGE STUDENTS: BRIDGING THE
CLASSROOM GAP TOGETHER
Vickie L. Harvey, Teresa Heinz Housel (eds.)
New Directions for Teaching and Learning, no. 127
Catherine M. Wehlburg, Editor-in-Chief

Microfilm copies of issues and articles are available in 16mm and 35mm,
as well as microfiche in 105mm, through University Microfilms, Inc.,
300 North Zeeb Road, Ann Arbor, MI 48106-1346.

NEW DIRECTIONS FOR TEACHING AND LEARNING (ISSN 0271-0633, elec-
tronic ISSN 1536-0768) is part of The Jossey-Bass Higher and Adult
Education Series and is published quarterly by Wiley Subscription
Services, Inc., A Wiley Company, at Jossey-Bass, 989 Market Street, San
Francisco, CA 94103-1741. Periodicals postage paid at San Francisco,
CA, and at additional mailing offices. POSTMASTER: Send address
changes to New Directions for Teaching and Learning, Jossey-Bass, 989
Market Street, San Francisco, CA 94103-1741.

New Directions for Teaching and Learning is indexed in CIJE: Current
Index to Journals in Education (ERIC), Contents Pages in Education
(T&F), Current Abstracts (EBSCO), Educational Research Abstracts
Online (T&F), ERIC Database (Education Resources Information
Center), Higher Education Abstracts (Claremont Graduate University),
and SCOPUS (Elsevier).

SUBSCRIPTIONS cost $89 for individuals and $275 for institutions, agencies,
and libraries in the United States. Prices subject to change.

EDITORIAL CORRESPONDENCE should be sent to the editor-in-chief,
Catherine M. Wehlburg, c.wehlburg@tcu.edu.

www.josseybass.com

CONTENTS

FROM THE SERIES EDITOR

About This Publication

Since 1980, *New Directions for Teaching and Learning* (NDTL) has brought a unique blend of theory, research, and practice to leaders in postsecondary education. NDTL sourcebooks strive not only for solid substance, but also for timeliness, compactness, and accessibility.

The series has four goals: to inform readers about current and future directions in teaching and learning in postsecondary education, to illuminate the context that shapes these new directions, to illustrate these new directions through examples from real settings, and to propose ways in which these new directions can be incorporated into still other settings.

This publication reflects the view that teaching deserves respect as a high form of scholarship. We believe that significant scholarship is conducted not only by researchers who report results of empirical investigations, but also by practitioners who share disciplinary reflections about teaching. Contributors to NDTL approach questions of teaching and learning as seriously as they approach substantive questions in their own disciplines. They deal both with pedagogical issues as well as the intellectual and social context in which these issues arise. Authors deal on the one hand with theory and research and on the other with practice, and they translate from research and theory to practice and back again.

About This Volume

This volume focuses on first-generation college students. These students often have to overcome many obstacles to successfully complete their degree program. Providing faculty with resources and answers to questions about first-generation students is essential. The research and the stories shared by the authors within this volume are fascinating, heart-touching, and important and will provide information and understanding to all who read it.

Catherine M. Wehlburg
Editor-in-Chief

CATHERINE M. WEHLBURG is the assistant provost for Institutional Effectiveness at Texas Christian University.

FOREWORD

Drawing on her thirteen years of experience as director of Indiana University-Bloomington's Groups Program, which serves first-generation and low-income students, the author details the challenges facing first-generation college students (FGS). She argues for the need for sourcebooks such as this one to educate higher-education personnel about the academic, cultural, and social experiences of FGS. Educating college and university personnel is the first step toward improving FGS' college success, retention, and graduation rates.

Faculty and First-Generation College Students: Bridging the Classroom Gap Together

Janice Wiggins

I have been the director of Indiana University-Bloomington's (IUB) Groups Program for more than thirteen years. I was also first in my family to attend college in the early 1960s, when I had little knowledge about what college would be like. I have worked with first-generation college students (FGS) and know intimately of the factors influencing their college preparation and success.

The first year of college is a crucial point for all students, but the transition to college can be particularly difficult for at-risk populations (Tinto, 1993). Tinto found that low-income, FGS experience the highest dropout rates and are more likely to leave after the first year. Pascarella and Terenzini (1991) suggest that the lower college performance and retention rates of low-income FGS are as likely to result from experiences *during* college as experiences students have *before* they enroll.

This volume is dedicated to Vickie L. Harvey's mother, Mary Ann Bertucci Plumley. She is the mother of a first-generation college student who earned a Ph.D. and full professorship with the heart of a working-class background.

NEW DIRECTIONS FOR TEACHING AND LEARNING, no. 127, Fall 2011 © Wiley Periodicals, Inc.
Published online in Wiley Online Library (wileyonlinelibrary.com) • DOI: 10.1002/tl.451

1

I recall a student's essay for admission to our program that showed the emotional challenges often encountered by FGS. She was concerned about leaving her family to attend a predominately white institution. She said:

> "Students with parents who can navigate the uncharted territory which college holds have an advantage that is difficult for us who are low income and first generation. We tend to straddle two cultures, that of the college community and that of our home environment. It is hard to stay positive when you feel you are unprepared or somehow feel inferior to your peers when you work just as hard as they do. It is hard to feel as though my education is comparable to that of those students from private and township schools. It's hard to stay positive in school when you know your parents could lose their job or home and you feel you are being selfish in neglecting family responsibility to pursue an education."

Emotional challenges are just one barrier to success for FGS. Our support program thus addresses the diverse challenges that FGS encounter in the areas of academic performance, learning, engagement, emotional well-being, and retention. Our Groups Program is a federal initiative of the U.S. Department of Education's Student Support Services Program, one of the Federal TRIO Programs that provide educational support for FGS. Our mission is to support, retain, and increase the graduation rates of first-generation, low-income, and disabled students. The Groups Program began as a pilot program in 1968 with forty-three students to address our low minority enrollment. Four decades later, more than 10,000 students from Indiana have participated, with more than 250 students enrolled every year.

What makes our program successful is its focus on the "whole student." Our holistic approach begins with the mandatory Summer Experience Program (SEP) component and continues with year-round support services. These services include intrusive academic advising, academic tutoring services, one-on-one and group mentoring, financial aid advising, peer instruction, psychological counseling, small learning group communities, arts exposure, and international travel experiences. Our recent endeavors include a male initiative providing support for cultural and social issues to address male retention, and a female initiative with mentoring for greater support and stability in an academic environment. We hope our program serves as a model for other FGS program initiatives.

This coedited volume greatly extends the scholarship on FGS. It is an honor to be asked by Teresa Heinz Housel, associate professor of communication at Hope College, and Vickie Harvey, professor of communication studies at California State University, Stanislaus, to write this foreword. Teresa taught FGS in our program's Summer Experience Program component in 2002. The experience vastly contributed to her growth and expertise as a professor, mentor, and advocate for FGS.

NEW DIRECTIONS FOR TEACHING AND LEARNING • DOI: 10.1002/tl

This volume's valuable research about the academic, cultural, and social experiences of FGS applies to a broad audience including faculty who teach and advise FGS, graduate students in higher education, university administrators, academic and student support services staff, high school teachers, and high school and college counselors.

In Chapter One, the editors discuss obstacles facing FGS and how the book's chapters address them. Section One (Chapters Two through Four) details how the trend of more FGS attending college is leading some to continue on to graduate school. However, the decision to pursue graduate study brings a new set of challenges as students navigate the unfamiliar maze of graduate school applications and adjusting to graduate academic culture. Section Two (Chapters Five through Nine) extends the existing FGS-related literature and uses original research such as surveys and qualitative interviews to discuss the complex interplay of social, academic, emotional, and financial influences on FGS' academic performance. The important influences include the impact of critical compassionate communication and pedagogy on student success; the impact of race and class on students' potential for college success, level of support networks, and college retention; barriers to success for Native American FGS, a first-generation demographic that has barely received scholarly attention; and reasons why FGS are dismissed from college and strategies for engaging readmitted students and preventing dismissals in the first place.

The chapters collectively affirm that the commitment of university resources is critical to college success. Institutions must fund programs promoting the continued retention and graduation success of first-generation and low-income students. Institutions should identify alternatives or develop creative funding to continue FGS support. Funding examples include department grants and fellowships, fundraising campaigns through university foundation and fundraising partners to provide scholarships and fellowships, and community partnerships providing resources to help finance the education and improve the college experiences of FGS.

As suggested by this volume's chapters, I believe more can be done to improve college retention and graduation rates of FGS at American colleges and universities. The chapters detail effective ways to accomplish this goal. Removing all barriers that deter underrepresented students is required to promote and accomplish the goals of student access, retention, and graduation. When we fulfill the mission to increase retention and graduation to support the long-term success of FGS, we will all win.

Janice Wiggins
Director/Groups Student Support Services
Indiana University, Bloomington

References

Pascarella, E. T., and Terenzini, P. T. *How College Affects Students*. San Francisco: Jossey-Bass, 1991.

Tinto, V. *Leaving College: Rethinking the Causes and Cures of Student Attrition*. (2nd ed.). Chicago: The University of Chicago, 1993.

JANICE WIGGINS *has been an administrator at Indiana University-Bloomington for more than twenty-five years. For the past thirteen years, she has been director of Groups Student Support Services at Indiana University. The Groups Program began in 1968 to increase the number of IU minority students. Partially funded by the federal government, each year it admits about 300 first-generation college students from Indiana without a parent who completed a four-year degree. About two-thirds of Groups students are black or Hispanic. Wiggins has also served on the Midwest Association of Education Opportunity Personnel Programs (MAEOPP) and the MAEOPP Education Foundation Board. In February 2009, Wiggins was honored as a Living Legend by the City of Bloomington for Black History Month.*

NEW DIRECTIONS FOR TEACHING AND LEARNING • DOI: 10.1002/tl

1

First-generation college students (FGS) often straddle different cultures between school and home. Because of this cultural disparity, FGS frequently encounter barriers to academic success and require additional support resources on campus. Simply offering more financial aid does not address the cultural and emotional challenges that these students experience. The volume's coeditors draw on their own first-generation college experiences to assert the necessity of this volume to assist college and university administrators, faculty, and staff who frequently work with FGS.

Introduction: Shall We Gather in the Classroom?

Teresa Heinz Housel, Vickie L. Harvey

In early 2008, Vanessa Greene, head of multicultural education at Hope College, and I (Teresa Housel) created a new program to mentor first-generation college students (FGS), whose parents do not have a bachelor's or an associate degree. We created the program out of the recognition that FGS encounter academic, cultural, emotional, and financial difficulties when attending college. FGS are an increasing student population at a time when employers are demanding a college degree even for an interview in an ever-tightening economy. According to a 2007 study by the University of California-Los Angeles's Higher Education Research Institute, nearly one in six freshmen at American four-year institutions are first-generation (Saenz and others, 2007). First-generation college students comprise a small demographic of our college's applicant pool, but their numbers are increasing as our institution expands its multicultural diversity program.

In an informal discussion group we established for our FGS, the students described the struggle to balance the demands of their new college environment with their familial backgrounds. Indeed, students who are first-generation commonly describe the experience of straddling the two different cultures of home and school. Each environment has its own cultural mores and social rules. Even though we acknowledge the tensions between the two milieus, we encouraged the students to use college resources and try new experiences. Several students in our support group described their excitement about studying abroad with the help of financial aid. One student recounted her excitement to travel by plane to places she had read about in Europe.

NEW DIRECTIONS FOR TEACHING AND LEARNING, no. 127, Fall 2011 © Wiley Periodicals, Inc.
Published online in Wiley Online Library (wileyonlinelibrary.com) • DOI: 10.1002/tl.452

Her excitement immediately transported me back to the fall of 1992 as I prepared to study in London for a semester. Born with a keen sense of adventure, I spent hours as a child looking at maps, and dreaming of places I would someday see. I worked five jobs in the summer of 1992 to save for the travel. I could barely contain my excitement while traveling for the first time by air from Newark, New Jersey, to London in early 1993. I wrote in my journal during my first day in Vauxhall, London, on February 2, 1993: "I am surprised by the reactions that I am having now to my surroundings. I always expected that when I came to Europe that I would be completely different, drawn to the romantic image of myself. But I feel like me, only in a different setting. The surroundings are real, tangible, as if I had simply moved from one of my rooms at home into another."

Although I felt comfortable traveling during that spring of 1993, I was not prepared for the culture shock I experienced among my own Oberlin College peers who studied abroad with me. Many classmates hosted parents who traveled to England for vacations or even long weekends. I was dumbfounded to discover that some of my friends' families even swapped houses with other families in other countries. For many of my peers, this was not their first trip abroad; some had experienced international sabbaticals with professoriate parents or simply took international summer vacations. My classmates' assumed cultural capital of fluency in European languages, travel experiences, and knowledge of art and theater would be unthinkable luxuries in my working-class upbringing. I read about such experiences in books.

As I write this introduction, I am ironically preparing for my fifth trip back to Britain to establish a new study abroad program with a sister institution in Liverpool. I have traveled through more than twenty countries and lived in two since 1993. I remain passionate about international travel and travel with ease between borders. I long since made peace with my working-class upbringing and now celebrate my ability to code-switch between different class cultures. However, the feeling of straddling the working-class and middle-class cultures never goes away.

Most FGS share similar stories of cultural straddling. We developed this volume to help college and university administrators, faculty, and staff who frequently work with FGS. It is not uncommon for college or university personnel to be from middle- or upper-class backgrounds. It certainly makes sense; many people who earn graduate degrees come from families with means and where education is a given, not a dream. As a result, academic personnel do not always understand why FGS struggle academically, socially, and emotionally.

Many institutions respond to their increasing numbers of first-generation applicants by offering generous financial aid programs to level out access to higher education. My college alma mater no longer admits students regardless of their financial need. However, the college now has a financial assistance program (Oberlin Access Initiative) that enables Pell

NEW DIRECTIONS FOR TEACHING AND LEARNING • DOI: 10.1002/tl

Grant–eligible students to receive loan-free financial aid packages. Financial aid, though, is just part of the equation because of the cultural transitions that FGS experience.

Of course, the specific difficulties experienced by FGS depend on their campus environments. My experience as a first-generation college student at an elite private and residential liberal arts college probably differs from that of FGS juggling a full-time job with studies at an urban commuter college. Reflecting this diversity, the institutions discussed in this book range across private liberal arts colleges, community colleges, and large universities in urban and rural settings.

Regardless of the differences across institutions, researchers repeatedly find that FGS enter college with more potential barriers to achievement than non-FGS. FGS often lack reading, writing, and oral communication skills, which frequently lead to poor retention rates (Ryan and Glenn, 2002/2003; Reid and Moore, 2008). Compared to their peers from middle- and upper-class economic backgrounds, FGS take part in fewer extracurricular organizations, campus cultural programs, internships, and career networking activities (Glenn, 2004; Moschetti & Hudley, 2008). Many researchers report that social networks are crucial for academic success, but FGS typically have lower levels of parental involvement in their education and they carry the burden of financial worries (Bui, 2002; McCarron & Inkelas, 2006).

Moreover, many FGS feel socially, ethnically, and emotionally marginalized on campus (Bui, 2002; Lundberg, Schreiner, Hovaguimian, and Miller, 2007; Francis and Miller, 2008). These challenges are usually the most difficult for institutions to identify because they typically result from unspoken cultural expectations and social mores. First-generation college students often lack social capital, such as exposure to cultural arts that wealthier students might take for granted. They must often navigate the unwritten social rules of their peers, professors, and academic administrators, many of whom come from middle- and upper-class backgrounds (Lubrano, 2004). Although I was a quick learner, in college I initially navigated unfamiliar cultural terrain without a map.

Given the difficulty FGS have in traversing academic culture, this volume responds to and extends the previous FGS-related research. For example, many existing studies examine the college experiences of first-generation undergraduates. The findings have helped institutions develop effective first-generation support programs. However, most studies do not analyze the cultural and academic transitions experienced by first-generation graduate students. It is important to fill this gap in higher education research because an increasing number of first-generation undergraduates are going on to graduate study.

To this end, this volume's first section, "The New Pattern: First-Generation College Students as Graduate Students," begins the volume by discussing this new trend in FGS populations. Brett Lunceford's chapter,

"When First-Generation Students Go to Graduate School," details the mistakes Lunceford made while applying to graduate school because he was not able to glean advice from family or his job supervisor (who had no experience with graduate school). Lunceford wrote his graduate school applications with no knowledge about the reputations of graduate school programs, the importance of having some conference presentation experience, or even what type of writing sample to include. The challenges experienced by first-generation graduate students, Lunceford points out, "are likely compounded when they pursue graduate education."

In Valerie Lester Leyva's chapter, "First-Generation Latina Graduate Students: Balancing Professional Identity Development with Traditional Family Roles" (Chapter Three), she discusses the little-examined tensions that Latina FGS experience. Latina FGS encounter demands between their professional roles and maintaining valued aspects of their ethnic affiliation. The chapter uses interviews with Latina FGS who are graduate students and juggling multiple roles as students, family members, parents, and gender roles while wrestling with multiple identities.

LaKresha Graham (Chapter Four) in "Learning a New World: Reflections on Being a First-Generation College Student and the Influence of TRIO Programs" emphasizes the TRIO programs' important role in supporting FGS as they navigate unfamiliar academic culture. Upward Bound, Student Educational Support Services, and the McNair Scholars program are increasingly important as more FGS pursue graduate studies.

This volume's Section Two, "First-Generation Students Join the Undergraduate Ranks," features student and faculty perspectives of FGS college experiences. In this section, authors present cutting-edge and new qualitative and quantitative research that extends the current understanding of FGS. In Chapter Five, "Faculty Perceptions of the First-Generation Student Experience and Programs at Tribal Colleges," Jacqueline J. Schmidt and Yemi Akande look at barriers to success facing students at tribal colleges, and offer recommendations for improved student services based on the authors' interviews with faculty at five tribal colleges.

In Chapter Six, "Understanding the First-Generation Student Experience in Higher Education Through a Relational Dialectic Perspective," Russell Lowery-Hart and George Pacheco Jr. use interviews and focus groups to examine the tensions FGS experience in campus culture. Their research clarifies that FGS straddle two different cultures of academic and home, with each culture sometimes at odds in terms of values.

Jennifer Brost and Kelly Payne examine interviews from academically dismissed FGS in their chapter, "First-Generation Issues: Learning Outcomes of the Dismissal Testimonial for Academically Dismissed Students in the Arts & Sciences" (Chapter Seven). Existing studies already show that FGS drop out of college at higher rates than non-FGS. Brost and Payne give readers an important view into what specific issues led the students to fail academically. The authors found that the experience of dismissal for FGS

NEW DIRECTIONS FOR TEACHING AND LEARNING • DOI: 10.1002/tl

differs from that of non-FGS in that FGS cited wrong course choices, inability to examine personal strengths and weaknesses, and not seeking academic help as reasons for dismissal. First-generation college students who appealed their institution's dismissal decision repeatedly indicated they would become more involved in campus and seek faculty contact; these points, Brost and Payne found, are crucial for FGS success.

In Chapter Eight, "A Social Constructionist View of Issues Confronting First-Generation College Students," Steve Coffman uses interviews with FGS to argue that race and class are two areas in which students experience tension when transitioning into campus culture. In addition, Coffman found that FGS with a family history of poor decision making often repeat these mistakes in college. Coffman also suggests that a strong social network plays a crucial role in helping students adjust to college. Institutions must strive to provide social support when it is lacking in the students' familial and peer relationships.

Social support and other forms of positive communication are continuing themes in Chapter Nine, "Critical Compassionate Pedagogy and the Teacher's Role in First-Generation Student Success." Richie Neil Hao's reflective chapter focuses on his efforts to use critical compassionate pedagogy in his classes. Informed by Rosenberg's (2003) concept of nonviolent communication, Hao's pedagogical perspective encourages educators to be critical of institutional and classroom practices that ideologically place underserved students at disadvantaged positions. At the same time, this perspective urges teachers to be self-reflective of their actions through compassion as a daily commitment. Hao suggests that this communication approach helps teachers counter institutional barriers and oppressive pedagogical practices that inhibit FGS success.

Our hope is that the new and cutting-edge research in this volume will help institutions create programs that better serve FGS. Learning communities are strengthened by including diverse student populations such as FGS, who have particular emotional, academic, and financial needs.

References

Bui, K. V. "First-Generation College Students at a Four-Year University: Background Characteristics, Reasons for Pursuing Higher Education, and First-Year Experiences." *College Student Journal,* 2002, *36*(1), 3–11.

Francis, T. A., and Miller, M. T. "Communication Apprehension: Levels of First-Generation College Students at 2-Year Institutions." *Community College Journal of Research and Practice,* 2008, *32*(1), 38–55.

Glenn, D. "For Needy Students, College Success Depends on More than Access, Study Finds." *The Chronicle of Higher Education,* 2004, *51*(2), p. A41.

Lubrano, A. *Limbo: Blue-Collar Roots, White-Collar Dreams.* Hoboken, N.J.: John Wiley & Sons, 2004.

Lundberg, C. A., Schreiner, L. A., Hovaguimian, K., and Miller, S. S. "First-Generation Status and Student Race/Ethnicity as District Predictors of Student Involvement and Learning. *NASPA Journal (Online),* 2007, *44*(1), 57–83.

McCarron, G. P., and Inkelas, K. K. "The Gap between Educational Aspirations and Attainment for First-Generation College Students and the Role of Parental Involvement." *Journal of College Student Development*, 2006, *47*(5), 534–549.

Moschetti, R., and Hudley, C. "Measuring Social Capital among First-Generation and Non-First-Generation, Working-Class, White Males. *Journal of College Admission*, 2008, *198*, 25–30.

Reid, M. J., and Moore, J. L. "College Readiness and Academic Preparation for Postsecondary Education: Oral Histories of First-Generation Urban College Students." *Urban Education*, 2008, *43*(2), 240–261.

Rosenberg, M. B. *Nonviolent Communication: A Language of Life.* (2nd ed.). Encinitas, Calif.: PuddleDancer Press, 2003.

Ryan, M. P., and Glenn, P. A. "Increasing One-Year Retention Rates by Focusing on Academic Competence: An Empirical Odyssey." *Journal of College Student Retention*, 2002/2003, *4*(3), 297–324.

Saenz, V. B., and others. *First in My Family: A Profile of First-Generation College Students at Four-Year Institutions since 1971.* Los Angeles: Higher Education Research Institute, 2007.

TERESA HEINZ HOUSEL *is an associate professor of communication at Hope College in Holland, Michigan. While a first-generation college student at Oberlin College in the early 1990s, she became interested in how the academic environment culturally marginalizes many FGS. Her research in the areas of homelessness; the politics of housing; media and globalization; and language, power, and class have appeared in* Critical Studies in Media Communication, Information, Communication & Society, *and* Journal of Critical Inquiry.

VICKIE L. HARVEY *is a full professor in the Communication Studies Department at the California State University, Stanislaus. She conducts research and teaches courses that emphasize the importance of communicating in relationships. Her primary line of research focuses on cross-sex friendships and how platonic friends meet O'Meara's four challenges of remaining just friends. She and Dr. Heinz Housel published their first book,* The Invisibility Factor: Administrators and Faculty Reach Out to First-Generation College Students *(BrownWalker Press), on first-generation college students and how administrative programs help FGS succeed in college. Her research has been published in* Sex Roles, Communication Teacher, Iowa Journal of Communication, The Qualitative Report, International Journal of Information and Communication Technology Education, The Academic Exchange Quarterly, *and* Readings in Gender Communication. *She is currently an editor for* The Academic Exchange Quarterly.

SECTION ONE

The New Pattern:
First-Generation College
Students as Graduate Students

2

The author argues that first-generation college students (FGS) have compounded challenges when they pursue graduate education. As a first-generation college student, he was not able to gather advice from family or his job supervisor, who had no experience with graduate school. Drawing from his experience and the existing FGS-related research, the author details practical advice for making a successful transition from college to graduate school. He concludes with a list of essential questions that prospective graduate students should ask themselves and their mentors when considering graduate study.

When First-Generation Students Go to Graduate School

Brett Lunceford

One of my graduate students recently asked me why I help them so much. The long answer involves my conception of what it means to be a professor and mentor to students. The short answer is that I have already made many mistakes that they might also make without the advice of someone who has been there.

I was the first in my family to earn a bachelor's degree, and I did not know anyone who had attended graduate school, so I applied to graduate school without really knowing the process. I decided to obtain my master's degree while working full time, so I only applied to the local university. I asked work colleagues to write recommendation letters. My boss had not attended college, so he made me write the letter with him—a process similar to the blind leading the blind. Fortunately, the school where I applied for my master's seemed to admit students who met the minimum requirements. This is not necessarily the case in doctoral programs or selective master's programs.

When I applied to doctoral programs, I made many mistakes. Because I planned to complete my master's degree in one year, my recommendation letters came from the three doctorate-holding professors I had taken that semester. This must have seemed a strange mix to the admissions committee because only one of these professors taught in the subject area for which I applied. In hindsight, my writing sample was awful and a poor choice. In my rhetoric program applications, I submitted a research proposal for an ethnographic study. I wrote one statement of purpose with

NEW DIRECTIONS FOR TEACHING AND LEARNING, no. 127, Fall 2011 © Wiley Periodicals, Inc.
Published online in Wiley Online Library (wileyonlinelibrary.com) • DOI: 10.1002/tl.453

13

little thought of adapting it to different programs. I had not presented research at academic conferences, nor did I know the professional organizations to which I should have belonged. I sent a résumé because I did not know what a curriculum vitae was. I obtained most information about graduate programs by finding them on the Internet and knew nothing of their reputations. Unaware that Iowa was one of my field's top programs, I applied to Iowa thinking that the program was probably not that desirable because of its location. I received advice even though I did not seek it out. My adviser suggested I apply to her doctoral alma mater, Penn State, which was the only school where I was accepted.

I provide this narrative to illustrate two points. First, just because we are dealing with graduate students or potential graduate students does not mean they understand what it means to be in the discipline or how graduate education works at other institutions. Second, when students are left to their own devices, they sometimes behave in ways that seem puzzling to those who know better—despite the internal logic of such behaviors—as they navigate a system of trial and error. Education researchers have found that FGS already have significant challenges in undergraduate education (Strayhorn, 2006; Collier and Morgan, 2008; Orbe, 2008; Merritt, 2008, 2010). These challenges are likely compounded when they pursue graduate education.

The subject of this chapter is how to best help FGS make the transition from college to graduate school. To this end, I address three different areas that build on each other: the period in which the student is considering graduate school, the process of applying to graduate school, and preparing the student for graduate school. I partially wrote this chapter to remind faculty of the processes and knowledge that we often take for granted. However, my main intention is to help students gain a clearer understanding of the process and know what questions to ask at each stage.

Contemplating Graduate School

Academic departments often have weak advising. Students are left to their own devices, armed only with a course catalogue and an online registration system. Advising should be more than helping students choose classes. Faculty should develop relationships with their advisees. Pragmatically, faculty needs to write recommendation letters regardless of whether students apply for graduate school. Second, advisers must be able to assess aptitude and desire for graduate studies. The first step to helping FGS who may go to graduate school is to know if graduate study is a likely path for them. This assessment is difficult to do without understanding the student's goals, desires, and values. Advising can come from not only the student's academic adviser, but also from another faculty mentor. For the remainder of this chapter, I will simply refer to that person as the student's mentor.

NEW DIRECTIONS FOR TEACHING AND LEARNING • DOI: 10.1002/tl

In my experience, students wishing to pursue graduate education frequently do not know if graduate study will enhance their chosen career. Some students think that they need a graduate degree when they may only need a bachelor's degree and internship/job experience. Goyette (2008) observes that the expectation that high school students will go on to attain a bachelor's degree "has, over the past twenty years, become the 'norm'" (p. 475). Consequently, many students conclude that they must pursue graduate school to stand out. However, graduate school is not always the best path. The student and mentor should thus together weigh the pros and cons of graduate school.

There are other issues mentors and students must consider in addition to the student's career and life goals. First, is the student willing to relocate to pursue a graduate degree? This will be discussed further in the next section, but there may be family considerations, such as caring for aging parents or the necessity of having a family support structure, that the student should consider.

Second, can the student handle the workload of advanced studies, especially with a teaching or research assistantship? In the humanities and social sciences, graduate students may teach two courses per semester in addition to their own studies. Science students may be part of a team that logs hundreds of laboratory hours. I was personally unprepared for the intensity of my doctoral program's workload. In fact, I thought that I had made a tremendous mistake and would fail all of my classes. I often had to read 200–300 pages per week in multiple classes each semester. In addition, my professors expected me to write at least one major research paper of conference quality for each class. Of course, there are less-rigorous programs, but even those require a significant time and energy investment. However, a student's status as a first-generation college student has less impact on his or her success than intelligence, stamina, and willingness to persevere.

Finally, the mentor should help the student understand the necessary training for the desired job. Graduate school has little benefit for some careers. In addition, some fields are saturated with highly qualified candidates and some universities have difficulty placing graduates because of inadequate training. There is also the issue of gaining appropriate training for the desired position. For example, my brother assumed he would need an MBA to practice business development, but he attended law school after discovering that most people in the field had law degrees.

Once a student has decided to pursue graduate education, the mentor can guide the student toward opportunities that will make him or her more desirable to graduate programs. For example, many universities have departmental committees that require student participation. The mentor can steer the student toward these opportunities or recommend him or her for the position. Students are often unaware of academic conferences where they can present their research. Some national and regional conferences encourage undergraduates to present in designated student sections. Of course, this requires that faculty provide research opportunities that demonstrate that the student is not simply a student, but an active and participating member of the discipline.

Applying to Graduate School

Once a student has decided to pursue graduate school, the mentor must guide him or her through a seemingly convoluted process with early deadlines. Students are sometimes surprised when they are told that the end of their senior year is too late to begin graduate school applications. It is therefore imperative to identify students wishing to go to graduate school well before their senior year. In addition, effective mentoring helps students realize that graduate and undergraduate admissions have different requirements. Students must take the required aptitude tests, such as the Graduate Record Examination (GRE), before they apply. Students should ideally take the exam early so they can retake it if higher scores are necessary.

The most important aspect of mentoring a student applying to graduate school is helping him or her select potential graduate programs. The mentor and student should carefully discuss the student's research interests to determine the best graduate programs. Most undergraduates have little understanding of different programs' strengths and weaknesses. Even exceptional programs cannot be all things to all people. Although a school's reputation may be a factor in selecting an undergraduate program, students often choose a graduate program to work with a particular adviser or scholar. Many undergraduates do not initially realize that graduate education thus resembles an apprenticeship.

In my experience, when FGS want to remain in a specific geographic location, this poses unique mentoring challenges. It is often difficult to explain that the programs that will best help the student meet his or her goals may be far away from family and friends. The student may be tied to a location by a spouse's job or by family obligations, and may be reluctant to uproot the family, especially if personal identity is rooted to the location. This situation requires both sensitivity to the student's feelings and honesty. If a nearby program is unlikely to fulfill the student's goals, it does little good to encourage enrollment. The best a mentor can do in this situation is to help the student weigh sometimes conflicting interests and desires.

Once the student and mentor have identified worthwhile graduate programs, the mentor should help the student craft an appropriate statement of purpose, curriculum vitae, and writing sample. Students often think of the statement of purpose as an autobiography. I encourage students to instead think of the statement from the standpoint of faculty members who will read the statement and ask questions such as, "Would I want to work with this person?" or "Why is this person applying here?" Faculty look for clues that will help them know if the student will be a valuable and successful member of the program.

NEW DIRECTIONS FOR TEACHING AND LEARNING • DOI: 10.1002/tl

Students often underestimate the importance of recommendation letters. Faculty members develop extensive professional networks through publishing, conference attendance, friends from graduate school, and other activities. These networks can be pivotal in the application process. I know a graduate student who was admitted to an excellent doctoral program. He had solid grades and presented research at conferences, but his GRE scores were below the required threshold. In competitive programs, there would be many candidates with the first two characteristics in addition to acceptable GRE scores. Yet this student obtained letters of recommendation from faculty with connections at the desired university. In addition to writing the letters, the faculty members called their friends at the other university and discussed the student. Because graduate education closely approximates an apprenticeship, departments are more likely to take a chance on a promising candidate recommended by a trusted friend, or at least someone that they know by reputation.

Unfortunately, in many universities large lecture courses are becoming the norm, making it difficult for students to develop relationships with faculty. In such situations, the impetus often lies with the student in developing these relationships. This can be done by discussing the material with the professor during office hours and participating in class. The student might also take multiple classes with the same professor if his or her area of expertise coincides with the student's interests.

If appropriate, it may be beneficial for the student to work with the mentor in an independent study that will help the student demonstrate the ability to conduct original research. First, independent study allows the mentor to assess the student's readiness for graduate school and identify areas needing improvement. Second, because many undergraduate courses do not encourage original research, an independent study provides an opportunity to create a writing sample that will showcase the student's research interests. Third, the project could be presented at a scholarly convention, which enhances the student's curriculum vitae.

Preparing for Graduate School

When students ask me what graduate school is like, I tell them about the beginning of the television show "Kung Fu," in which a monk has to move an iron cauldron filled with burning coals from one fire to the other with his bare arms pressed against strategically placed dragons. After completing this task, he thrusts his arms into the snow to stop the burning. I explain that graduate school is similar: "It will be painful, you'll be scarred for life, and you'll never again be the same—but you'll have some bitchin' dragons on your arms to show for it."

The capacity to succeed in college seems to be related more to involvement or aspiration than to first-generation status (Pascarella, Pierson, Wolniak, and Terenzini, 2004; Pike and Kuh, 2005; Strayhorn, 2006).

NEW DIRECTIONS FOR TEACHING AND LEARNING • DOI: 10.1002/tl

It seems reasonable to concede that this is likely the case for FGS who attend graduate school. Yet there is more to graduate education than simply being able to do the work. Graduate school is doubly difficult for students lacking a passion for knowledge that will sustain them though the difficulties that inevitably arise. Therefore, the most important thing that faculty can do to prepare FGS for graduate school is to inculcate a love of the material (Espinoza-Herold and Gonzalez, 2007; Próspero and Vohra-Gupta, 2007).

I have seen several students leave graduate programs because they did not have a burning question that would sustain them through their coursework, thesis, or dissertation. Of course, faculty should help the students find the material engaging. This may include helping students find opportunities for presenting their research at conferences and submitting it for publication. However, to help students develop a love for the material, faculty must also *demonstrate* a love for it. Helping students enjoy the material is an essential strategy for success even when dealing with FGS who do not wish to pursue graduate education.

Another way that students can prepare for graduate school is to become more knowledgeable about their chosen research area. In graduate school the required readings are merely the beginning; it is assumed students will seek out additional readings that will help them in their research. The readings will become much more intense in graduate school, and textbooks that condense and synthesize the subject matter for the reader will largely become outdated. Students will need to become familiar with the language of their chosen field by reading original research in journal articles and scholarly books. In addition to learning content, students should develop an orientation to their chosen discipline (Lunceford, 2009).

Finally, the student should begin developing a research agenda. After all, a graduate degree is a research degree. There is no reason why the student cannot begin participating in research activities as an undergraduate, and some schools actively encourage faculty to involve undergraduate students in research. The student should discuss with the mentor opportunities to participate in a research project or the possibility of doing an independent study. In this way, the student can begin to see how his or her research agenda fits into the field's larger scholarly discourse. This is the beginning of the transition from an undergraduate mentality to that of a graduate student where one becomes not only a consumer of knowledge, but also a producer.

Conclusion

Because more students in general are pursuing graduate studies, it is therefore likely that many FGS will also become graduate students. The issues confronting them as undergraduates—integration, employment status, family situation—will be just as pressing, if not more so, in graduate school. Faculty must be prepared to discuss the pros and cons of graduate school with these students in a way that acknowledges their life situations, yet also provides an honest assessment of how graduate school will further affect their lives.

To summarize, students should ask the following questions of themselves and their mentors:

1. Would graduate school help me attain my goals?
2. What should I do to maximize my chances of admission to graduate school?
3. What schools would best serve my interests, and am I willing to relocate to go to one of them?
4. Am I prepared to invest the necessary time and energy to succeed in graduate studies?

Once these questions have been carefully considered and honestly answered, the student can then discuss with the mentor the process of applying to graduate schools, as each discipline has its own quirks. Ideally, the student should begin this process well before the senior year to develop a network of faculty members willing to assist in the application process and to gain research opportunities.

Graduate school is a difficult experience that is often compounded when the student comes from a family uninformed concerning the intricacies of graduate education. First-generation graduate students may not know where to get the information that will help them succeed, and processes that faculty take for granted can seem an impenetrable maze to students. As we help FGS make the transition to college, faculty must recognize that for many of them an undergraduate degree is only the beginning of their experience in academia. With appropriate guidance, it is likely that many of them may become not only our students, but our future colleagues as well.

References

Collier, P., and Morgan, D. "Is That Paper Really Due Today?: Differences in First-Generation and Traditional College Students' Understandings of Faculty Expectations." *Higher Education,* 2008, 55(4), 425–446.

Espinoza-Herold, M., and Gonzalez, V. "The Voices of Senior Scholars on Mentoring Graduate Students and Junior Scholars." *Hispanic Journal of Behavioral Sciences,* 2007, 29(3), 313–335.

Goyette, K. A. "College for Some to College for All: Social Background, Occupational Expectations, and Educational Expectations over Time." *Social Science Research,* 2008, 37(2), 461–484.

Lunceford, B. "In Defense of Teaching 'Outdated' Material." *ETC: A Review of General Semantics,* 2009, 66, 263–268.

Merritt, C. R. "First-Generation College Students: Then and Now." *Human Architecture: Journal of the Sociology of Self-Knowledge,* 2008, 6(1), 45–51.

Merritt, C. R. "Accommodating the First-Generation College Student." *National Social Science Journal,* 2010, *33*(2), 121–125.

Orbe, M. P. "Theorizing Multidimensional Identity Negotiation: Reflections on the Lived Experiences of First-Generation College Students." In M. Azmitia, M. Syed, and K. Radmacher (eds.), *The Intersections of Personal and Social Identities.* New Directions for Child and Adolescent Development, no. 120. San Francisco: Jossey-Bass, 2008.

Pascarella, E. T., Pierson, C. T., Wolniak, G. C., and Terenzini, P. T. (2004). "First-Generation College Students: Additional Evidence on College Experiences and Outcomes." *Journal of Higher Education,* 2004, *75*(3), 249–284.

Pike, G. R., and Kuh, G. D. (2005). "First- and Second-Generation College Students: A Comparison of Their Engagement and Intellectual Development." *Journal of Higher Education,* 2005, *76*(3), 276–300.

Próspero, M., and Vohra-Gupta, S. "First Generation College Students: Motivation, Integration, and Academic Achievement." *Community College Journal of Research & Practice,* 2007, *31*(12), 963–975.

Strayhorn, T. L. "Factors Influencing the Academic Achievement of First-Generation College Students." *NASPA Journal,* 2006, *43*(4), 82–111.

BRETT LUNCEFORD *was the first in his family to complete college, as well as the first to complete graduate education. Since he earned his B.S. in speech communication, both his mother and brother have gone back to school to complete a B.A. in liberal studies and a B.S. in computer science and a J.D., respectively. In his current position as assistant professor of communication at the University of South Alabama, Brett is especially interested in helping new graduate students navigate the often unspoken assumptions surrounding graduate education. In doing so, he hopes to help others avoid the mistakes that he made along the way. His work has appeared in* American Communication Journal, Communication Teacher, ETC: A Review of General Semantics, Explorations in Media Ecology, Media History Monographs, Northwestern Journal of Technology and Intellectual Property, Review of Communication, *and* Theology and Sexuality.

NEW DIRECTIONS FOR TEACHING AND LEARNING • DOI: 10.1002/tl

3

The author discusses the little-examined tensions that female and Latina first-generation college students (FGS) experience while negotiating their ethnic and professional identities. Despite having general parental support for pursuing an education, Latina and female FGS who are graduate students in the author's university department must juggle multiple identities of gender role expectations with being students, family members, and parents.

First-Generation Latina Graduate Students: Balancing Professional Identity Development with Traditional Family Roles

Valerie Lester Leyva

Despite the best intentions of most parents to prepare their children for adult success, their efforts do not always result in initially sustainable efforts. In my family, the usual path led to military service with the hope of learning a trade or some other employable skill. From an early age, however, it was clear that my life journey would lead me to a college degree.

Throughout my years in high school, my parents provided me with support and encouragement. Their graduation gifts to me of a Smith Corona manual typewriter and a 1971 Chevy Impala with a rebuilt engine were intended to set me on course to academic and social success. Even with their love and best wishes, and their fervent desire that I become a successful college-educated woman, it soon became clear that I was woefully underprepared.

Although my parents valued education, the culture of my working-class family did not expose me to the stratified social structure and expectations of the large state university I attended. I was not prepared for the competing demands on my time, the difficulties of providing for my own financial support, the rigorous demands of my chosen academic program, and a very stressful and financially burdensome set of social expectations. This lack of preparation resulted in the necessity of taking a semester off to improve my financial standing and reconsider my career plans. After this time of reflection and gainful employment, and consolidation of my college experiences with my family's profound lack of understanding of the processes of higher education, I returned to college with a more realistic and practical set of expectations.

My experiences as a first-generation college student, however, can be viewed from a particular standpoint: I am white, my family emigrated to the United States many generations ago, English is my first language, my parents demonstrated a fairly balanced set of gender role expectations, and my family expected me to attend college. Although I came from a context grounded in the dominant paradigm of experience in the United States, I still struggled to accommodate the expectations of college and professional identity development. This realization led me to consider the experiences of those who differ from this paradigm and have profoundly different cultural expectations. How do their experiences differ from mine? How is their identity shaped by the competing demands of maintaining valued aspects of their ethnic affiliation and negotiating successful professional roles?

To answer these questions, I looked to the student population that makes up the largest first-generation college student demographic group in the university department where I am employed. Latinas, more specifically, Mexican-American women, represent nearly 25 percent of the students in this Master of Social Work (MSW) program. All are FGS and are the first in their families to attend a graduate program.

My ability to access this group and the frank conversations they recounted were based on multiple factors. My interest in this population was generated by "parking lot" conversations after class with numerous Latina first-generation college students (FGS) regarding their ongoing negotiation of gender and familial roles subsequent to earning a college degree. One such student likened this process to metaphorically taking her house apart, brick by brick, and building a new structure that accommodated her new identity. It was clear that this process of role negotiation required significant thought and emotional energy and was profoundly transformative. Other factors that facilitated my access to this population were my history of acknowledging the complexity of Latin American ethnic identity in the United States and my personal struggles with being a first-generation college student.

After establishing the desire to tell their stories, a series of in-depth interviews was conducted with six Latina FGS MSW graduates. The interviews took place in dyads via facilitated conversations between the participants and lasted from 1.5 to 2.5 hours. Encouraging the participants to engage each other in dialogue, versus a more traditional researcher–participant interviewing method, stimulated discussion of a broader range of issues than originally conceptualized for this project. The interviews generated significant detail when the members of the dyad were good friends or colleagues; it was clear they had already undertaken many of these conversations. Each interview was audio recorded and transcribed. The data were

NEW DIRECTIONS FOR TEACHING AND LEARNING • DOI: 10.1002/tl

analyzed for themes using Neuman and Kreuger's (2003) method for qualitative data analysis.

The participants ranged in age from late 20s to late 50s. Two participants were born in Mexico and migrated to the United States in early childhood. All others were born in California but indicated that both parents were born either in Mexico or in towns on the U.S.–Mexico border. Most participants' families entered the United States to engage in migrant farm work. None of their parents or grandparents attended college; few even attended or graduated from high school. All participants earned a MSW degree from the same public university in central California. All were employed or actively seeking employment utilizing their social work credentials.

The starting point for discussions of negotiating identity became immediately apparent when participants related the terms each used to identify her ethnic affiliation. This question was embedded in a discussion of the reasons for choosing the term *Latina* for this project. When asked how she identified herself, one participant stated ". . . we could have this conversation for six hours." The terms participants used included Mexican, Mexican American, Latina, Hispanic, and Chicana. Each answer came with significant discussion regarding the politics of ethnic identity, the effect of ethnic terminology on personal identity and family dynamics, and the ways in which obtaining a college degree shifted or strengthened ethnic identity.

Most participants related how a firm ethnic identity was transmitted intergenerationally. When ethnicity was identified by family members, it was clearly termed *Mexican American*.

"I was raised to be specifically told that I am Mexican American. It's how I was identified by my family and how I was encouraged to call myself with my friends."

"That's what my grandfather said, 'you are Mexican American.'"

This is consistent with the *hyphenated-American* construction of ethnic terminology used by numerous groups of immigrants in the United States. Multiple researchers, however, describe the problems associated with treating Latino/as as members of a homogeneous group (Jones-Correa and Leal, 1996). Some participants rejected the notion of a monolithic term for all Spanish heritage people, such as Latino/a or Hispanic, while others found these terms more useful.

"For me Latina or Hispanic is nothing. It's too general."

"I just have to say it's only been the last few years that I've been okay with Latina or Hispanic."

NEW DIRECTIONS FOR TEACHING AND LEARNING • DOI: 10.1002/tl

"I say Hispanic. When I was younger I was forced to acculturate a little bit more. I've always had issues with my own . . . identity."

"I call myself Latina, because for me, the term Latina means I am from both [Mexico and the United States]."

Most participants acknowledged the amount of reflection and insight required to bridge two or more sets of ethnic identities. The motif of *border-land* and the liminal space occupied by Latino/as living between these two worlds is an essential feature of the identities negotiated by the participants in this study. For most, this issue began when attempting to negotiate the differences between those in their families who identify as Mexican and those who identify as Mexican American. These differences were based on various factors, ranging from country of birth and language usage to issues of skin complexion and cultural identification. All resulted in the necessity to develop a liminal identity characterized by statements of not quite fitting into either Mexican or American ethnicities.

"It's never Mexican and it's never American. For me I'm a blending of both of those."

"[F]or us who have emigrated, we [are] kind of a half and half. It's kind of mixed in together."

"I've met some people who have gone to school in Mexico, and they speak [Spanish] differently. It's a different culture there."

"I was not accepted completely by my dad's family . . . [t]hey called us the white people. We had such issues with that."

These women reside in the liminal, in-between space of *Mexican* and *American* that researchers identify as first-generation college student Latino/as (Ceballo, 2004; Ong, Phinney, and Dennis, 2006; Wilkinson, 2008). One factor is the influence of parents on first-generation college student Latino/a college completion. It is considered a significant factor in almost all research about this population. Ceballo identified three parenting characteristics common among successful first-generation Latino/a college students: a strong parental commitment to education, parental facilitation of the child's autonomy regarding the college search and choice process, and numerous nonverbal expressions of support for the child's educational achievement. Arellano and Padilla (1996) identified numerous factors accounting for Latino/a student success. In addition to general support for their academic pursuits and encouragement to succeed, working-class Latino/a parents support their child's educational attainment by instilling the notion that education is the path to economic and social success. Ong, Phinney, and Dennis also suggest that parental support for educational achievement may moderate the effects of low socio-economic status and is a strong, predictive factor for academic success.

The role of parental influence functioned similarly for many participants in this study. Most experienced valuable positive support and encouragement from parents and other family members. Academic achievement in the form of high school and college completion was framed as a path out of poverty. A few participants, however, encountered either significant opposition to or general apathy about their educational plans. This opposition seemed to form around socio-economic issues and expectations. One participant's family saw her attempts to attend college as a way to get out of work. Several participants recounted similar challenges. These attitudes point to the substantial pressure participants faced to abandon efforts at college completion and contribute to building financial assets for their families.

"My mother would say, 'You're the only one [in the family] who knows the English language, but you don't have a house and you don't have a car. You need to stop playing around. It's kind of like an excuse for you to not go to work.'"

"Even though I've always had their support, there's always been this undercurrent of 'how is it that you don't have a house,' or 'how is it that you don't have a car?'"

Several other participants indicated that their families, while supportive, did not have the expectation that they would finish high school, let alone college. "For me it was hoped I would graduate from high school, but my brothers, they didn't even graduate from high school. It was just, you should graduate. Who tells their children 'you should graduate'? That shouldn't even be an option, that should be a given."

Mixed in with both the support for and ambivalence about high school and college completion was a significant thread of parental confusion about the process of college itself. Course schedules, assignments, internships, and socializing with classmates were elements of a world participants' parents did not comprehend.

"But even then with my parents there was always this undercurrent of doubts and questions. 'What do you mean you're going to class at three in the afternoon? Don't they close the school at two?'"

"They do not understand about units. They do not understand about midterms. They don't understand about research papers and how long it takes to write them."

"With regards to thesis work, my mom doesn't understand. She just says 'why can't you get the damn thing done?'"

"My parents gave me the encouragement to attend college, but I didn't get much encouragement for the ups and downs."

The incongruity of encountering support, ambivalence, and confusion from their families regarding their educational goals led these participants to reflect on issues of *belonging*. The fundamental dualities they experienced across multiple domains of identity, including ethnicity and education, left them considering the ways in which these dualities affected how they fit into the social milieu at home and at work. They were clear that achieving college completion would increase their lifelong earning potential and provide a sound financial basis for marriage and children. However, they encountered considerable difficulties negotiating identities that resulted in a goodness-of-fit between professional and personal roles.

All participants commented on the demands of living in the liminal space between traditional Mexican, gender-based role expectations, and the interpersonal skills required in professional social work practice. In this task, they are not alone. Parra (2007) and Richter (2007) describe the challenges faced by Latinas who wish to obtain the benefits resulting from completion of a college-degree program and who are also bound by traditional gender-based family role expectations. Jezzini, Guzman, and Grayshield (2008) explore the concept of *marianismo* and its role in the lives of Mexican-American female college students. The phenomenon of marianismo ". . . encompasses sacred duty to family, subordination to men, subservience, selflessness, self renouncement and self sacrifice, chastity before marriage, sexual passivity after marriage, and erotic repression" (para. 9). This concept is used to bind women to their roles as servants and caretakers of the family (Marsiglia and Holleran, 1999). In particular, the themes of serving, anticipating the needs of men, and submission to men were embedded in all participants' descriptions of family gender role expectations.

The theme of *serving* others, particularly father and husband, was quite persistent. Participants described a firm expectation that a woman's role in the family was to cater to one's husband and male children. Participants recounted how serving was also used as a measure of a woman's intrinsic worth and how it affected the status of the family within the community. Failure to live up to this ideal appeared to be a source of shame.

"I remember my mom getting up at four o'clock in the morning to make tortillas and make [my Dad's] burritos."

"My mom used to give my dad a bath, cut his toe nails, I mean really groom him. She said she was a reflection of how he looked."

"Sometimes [my husband] washes dishes. My mom says, 'do not tell *anybody* that he washes the dishes.'"

"My brothers and my cousins . . . they continued to be babied because they were the males of the family and didn't really have to wash the dishes. They didn't have to wash their clothes."

"My mother came to visit me when my boys were coming up and she saw one of them washing dishes and she got pretty angry. 'Why are you allowing him to do that,' she said. 'That's women's work.'"

The expectation that participants would continue in the serving role was typically reinforced by their mothers and other female family members. All participants cited dissatisfaction with this role, and many actively challenged their mothers' expectations. Despite this, they all discussed the emotional toll it took to maintain more-balanced relationships with husbands and boyfriends and break out of these intergenerationally transmitted role expectations.

The gender-based role of *anticipating needs* was articulated by several participants. An element of the serving role, participants described the assumption that they would anticipate the needs of the men in the family and provide it before being asked.

"My dad's going to get home. My husband is going to get home. Let me wash some clothes because I know he's going to need them."

"At home you are cooking, you are cleaning, you are washing the clothes. You are guessing what they need before they walk in the door."

The final theme, *submission*, was a common refrain in participants' comments and completes the paradigm of servitude epitomized in marianismo, "It's the concept of being submissive; it's your role in the house." Submission ties Latinas to a model of behavior that results in a surrender of identity and a negation of self. This is most evident in the words of one participant as she describes her mother's relationship to her father, "'We've done everything . . . the way [your father] wanted because he was the provider of the family . . . He's the provider [and] I am his possession.'"

Attempts to integrate a professional social work identity with the firmly embedded cultural values of serving, anticipating needs, and submission was quite challenging for all first-generation college student Latina participants. The most difficult element of this work was to maintain the positive aspects of their cultural foundations while integrating professional social work values. It is not coincidental that this group of participants chose a profession characterized by service to others. However, professional social work has developed guidelines for ethical practice that assisted the participants to incorporate professional practice values into their personal schemas of what it means to serve others.

The guiding document for the professional practice of social work is the Code of Ethics (National Association of Social Workers, 1999). One of the foundational values articulated in this document is client self-determination and autonomy. This requires the social worker to place primary importance on the client's stated goals, rather than on any sense that the worker "knows what's best" for the client. It includes open dialogue with clients to identify their strengths and resources. It precludes the notions of serving or anticipating needs as participants have described it in their family contexts. Integrating this professional value with the gender-based role expectations was challenging for most participants. They indicated experiencing significant tension between their roles at home and the professional expectation that clients will take the lead in determining what they want and need: "You almost feel this power or force pulling you to tell [clients] 'you need to do this or that.' [Social workers] like helping out people, but at the same time you need to rein that back because you just want to do what you've been taught all your life, about how to be the server, how to be the one to [anticipate needs]."

While learning to mitigate the effects of the serving/anticipating role at work was challenging, by far the most difficult task in balancing the gender-based role expectations of a first-generation college student Latina and professional social work focused on the marianismo concept of submission. All participants commented on the stress of negotiating these two worlds, one in which she is expected to be submissive at home and assertive in the workplace. Most participants reported significant difficulty learning how to stand up to authority figures and speak up for clients and self, and experienced significant stress while learning to take on an assertive role, even when to advocate for others.

"If I disagree with [my supervisor] on the direction a case should take, because she is the supervisor, it is very hard for me to stand up and say what I believe in. It's almost like I'm disrespecting her."

"It is so hard to own up and let everybody see that you are a professional. Because all of your insecurities come up, because you are always used to seeing them as your superiors."

"I feel guilty for being assertive."

"Any time I have interactions with [a particular male coworker] I can't talk, and I feel like I have no brain. It's as if my experiences growing up are coming out and are impacting my work."

NEW DIRECTIONS FOR TEACHING AND LEARNING • DOI: 10.1002/tl

"It is so hard to operate in two different worlds. In one of the worlds you are supposed to be submissive, you are supposed to fulfill your role as a woman. Then you go to a world . . . where you have to say your [professional] opinion."

These participants employed multiple strategies to negotiate the boundaries between these two worlds. Some conceptualized this task as shifting between two cultures and likened it to wearing different masks for different roles.

"Your role is almost like you need to cook and clean and do your woman duties, whatever it is, what is expected of you, and then when you go into the professional arena, you have to wear a different mask."

"When you are sitting at a meeting with other professionals, it is so hard to mentally put that mask on your professionalism."

Rather than maintaining the dual identity of submissive/assertive in different arenas, some participants chose to move out of the submissive role altogether. To support this effort they relied on a network of similarly educated peers who have struggled with the same issues. These informal networks of first-generation college student Latinas offered a place to share common experiences, process feelings, and challenge one another to negotiate the nuances of a profession that requires claiming one's personal authority. Those who participated in these networks reported challenging each other to advocate for their own needs in the workplace and to resist being submissive to supervisors and other authority figures.

"I told her, 'when are you going to stand up for you, and when are you going to stand up for your staff?'"

"There is a point where you need to speak up for yourself because it's no longer about the job. It's about your dignity."

All of the Latina FGS in this project articulated the difficulties of living between two worlds: Mexican and American, family support for education and ambivalence, marianismo and professional social work practice. They have a lifetime of experience negotiating identity and living in the boundary between the two. Just as their mothers transmitted cultural expectations to them, so are they transmitting cultural expectations to their children.

However, the message has shifted. Most articulated a desire to place family at the center of their lives, but with more-balanced expectations regarding the roles of men and women. They want their children, both sons and daughters, to graduate from college. They describe marrying husbands who want their daughters to see men doing what is traditionally considered women's work. They teach their sons and daughters that women can be strong and independent, and that they deserve to be loved and treated with respect.

It is the hope of these Latina FGS that in telling their stories, they expand the circle of Mexican-American women who are struggling with the same issues. It is important to them that their Latina peers know it is possible to successfully negotiate a professional identity *and* maintain cultural values that focus on family ties and ethnic affiliation. Finally, it is crucial to them to transmit the essence of these negotiated roles to their children. As one participant stated, "I just hope that they see me as a woman who is caring and strong and pursuing dreams."

Her words represent the dreams of a generation.

References

Arellano, A., and Padilla, A. "Academic Invulnerability among a Select Group of Latino University Students." *Hispanic Journal of Behavioral Sciences,* 1996, *18*(4), 485–508.

Ceballo, R. "From Barrios to Yale: The Role of Parenting Strategies in Latino Families." *Hispanic Journal of Behavioral Sciences,* 2004, *26*(2), 171–186.

Jezzini, A., Guzman, C., and Grayshield, L. "Examining the Gender Role Concept of *Marianismo* and Its Relation to Acculturation in Mexican-American College Women." Paper presented at the VISTA: Proceedings of the ACA Annual Conference & Exhibition, Honolulu, Hawaii, March 2008. Retrieved from http://counselingoutfitters .com/vistas/vistas08/Jezzini.htm.

Jones-Correa, M., and Leal, D. "Becoming "Hispanic": Secondary Panethnic Identification Among Latin American-Origin Populations in the United States." *Hispanic Journal of Behavioral Sciences,* 1996, *18*(2), 214–254.

Marsiglia, F., and Holleran, L. "'I've Learned So Much from My Mother: Narratives from a Group of Chicana High School Students." *Social Work in Education,*1999, *21*(4), 220–237.

National Association of Social Workers. *Code of Ethics.* Washington, D.C.: National Association of Social Workers, 1999. Retrieved from http://www.socialworkers.org/ pubs/Code/code.asp.

Neuman, W. L., and Kreuger, L. *Social Work Research Methods: Qualitative and Quantitative Approaches.* Boston, Mass.: Pearson Education, 2003.

Ong, A., Phinney, J., and Dennis, J. Competence under Challenge: Exploring the Protective Influence of Parental Support and Ethnic Identity in Latino College Students. *Journal of Adolescence,* 2006, *29*, 961–979.

Parra, M. (2007). *Sociocultural, Resilience, Persistence and Gender Role Expectation Factors that Contribute to the Academic Success of Hispanic Females* (Doctoral dissertation). Available from ProQuest Dissertation and Theses database. (UMI No. 3274948).

Richter, B. (2007). *The Motivations and Support Systems of First-Generation Hispanic Community College Female Students* (Doctoral dissertation). Available from ProQuest Dissertation and Theses database. (UMI No. 3301738).

Wilkinson, L. (2008). *Inconsistent Hispanic/Latino Self-Identification in Adolescence and Academic Performance* (Doctoral dissertation). Available from ProQuest Dissertation and Theses database. (UMI No. 3320622).

VALERIE LESTER LEYVA is an assistant professor of social work at California State University, Stanislaus. She earned her Ph.D. in pastoral counseling from Loyola University in Baltimore, Maryland, a M.S.W. from the University of Maryland, a M.A. in theological studies from Wesley Theological Seminary, and a B.A. in history from the University of South Carolina. Dr. Leyva has several areas of active research. Her current interests include social service disparities among immigrant and undocumented workers in the agricultural industry; the availability of social support services for lesbian, gay, bisexual, and transgender individuals and families; and the intersections between social work and spirituality. All her work is formed by a commitment to social justice and based upon recognizing the dignity of all people.

4

As an African-American woman growing up in a working-class neighborhood, the author initially did not have mentors who could guide her successfully to college. However, the TRIO programs professionally and personally prepared Graham for higher education and an academic career.

Learning a New World: Reflections on Being a First-Generation College Student and the Influence of TRIO Programs

LaKresha Graham

What do you do if you have a dream, but do not know how to achieve it? And worse, what if you have no idea that you do not know how to achieve this dream? Well, TRIO programs exist for students like me—desiring higher education, but needing guidance through the academic systems that exist. As an African-American woman growing up in a working-class neighborhood, I did not have many personal connections with people who went to college. Unless people have been through higher education, they do not understand the nuances for getting accepted and graduating from college. Through TRIO programs, I found support to realize my educational goals.

TRIO programs began in 1964, when Lyndon Johnson signed the Educational Opportunity Act into law (McElroy and Armesto, 1998). This started the TRIO programs to help disadvantaged students enroll and complete college. TRIO programs, including Talent Search and Educational Opportunity Centers, help students get into undergraduate colleges and universities. I participated in the Upward Bound College Prep program, which prepares students for college through intensive on-campus classes and experiences, and the Ronald E. McNair Postbaccalaureate Program, which prepares underrepresented and first-generation college students (FGS) for graduate education and college-level teaching (Coles, 1998).

My involvement with TRIO began my freshman year of high school when my godsister suggested that I start Upward Bound with her. At this

NEW DIRECTIONS FOR TEACHING AND LEARNING, no. 127, Fall 2011 © Wiley Periodicals, Inc.
Published online in Wiley Online Library (wileyonlinelibrary.com) • DOI: 10.1002/tl.455

time, my godsister had spent the last two summers in Wichita, Kansas, in the Upward Bound Math and Science Program. When she would return from her summers away, she told stories about the friends she made and her experiences living in the dormitory. From her description, the idea of living the college life sounded fun and exciting (especially because I was in high school). I thought it would be great to join her there.

After talking with my high school counselor, I found out that there was an Upward Bound College Prep program at Saint Louis University (SLU), in my hometown, which I could participate in the next year. While my godsister left in the summer to live on campus and take classes in statistics, entomology, and other math and science-focused classes, the Upward Bound College Prep program was different. The SLU Upward Bound also offered college prep classes in English (such as literature and composition), math (algebra, pre-calculus, and statistics), and science (chemistry, biology, and physics) during the academic school year. There was tutoring for these classes, which helped me learn the material and maintain my grade point average (GPA) at my regular high school.

The program also included a summer component. By participating in the program, I was exposed to people from different backgrounds. Students came from the St. Louis metropolitan area, but also other cities in Missouri, Kansas, and Illinois. There were so many activities, such as going to see musicals and baseball games, which kept us entertained and enriched us. Contrary to college life, there was not much flexibility and freedom. Every minute, whether waking up at 7 a.m., meals, classes, tutoring, lights out, or "free time," was structured. A resident adviser, teacher, or administrator always knew our whereabouts; we were restricted in going to certain areas of campus (the residence hall, cafeteria, classes, library, or the gym); and we were never allowed to go anywhere by ourselves.

Even though these summers did not provide the carefree flexibility that college normally offers, the classes prepared us for college. I got used to being away from my family and relying on residential advisers and administrators to provide guidance. I know that much of the structure of Upward Bound was because we were minors, but this arrangement forced us to focus on studying. This showed me the amount of time and energy it would take to be successful in college. Later, when I did start college, I knew that the flexible time between classes and activities was meant for studying.

During the school year, we also worked on other aspects of applying to college. Due to the necessity of standardized tests in college admissions, Upward Bound provided ACT preparation classes during my senior year. Instead of focusing on academic skills and content, instructors developed our test-taking skills (Allensworth, Correa, and Ponisciak, 2008). I learned how to dismiss incorrect answers rather than just looking for the correct one. Also, they showed me many times the answer was already in the exam. For example, in solving math problems, sometimes I could use the options

NEW DIRECTIONS FOR TEACHING AND LEARNING • DOI: 10.1002/tl

given to find the answer, especially if I was not sure how to complete the equation.

Upward Bound also held workshops on filling out the Free Application for Federal Student Aid (FAFSA) attended by students and parents. The FAFSA, a necessary step to get scholarships, grants, and loans, was difficult to figure out on my own. I had to complete the form to afford college. Completing the FAFSA was complicated, to say the least. Students needed to collect documentation before filling out the application (W-2 forms, bank statements, and any other income forms). Figuring out the necessary information for some questions was hard, especially for a 17-year-old who had not yet filed taxes. Many questions asked about gross income, savings, and investments. Then I had my own questions. Should I only include my mother's income, or add the income from my part-time job? How do I show on the form that there are two different incomes? I felt pressured to make everything perfect and kept thinking about if I would be able to even afford college.

My biggest concern occurred after the application was filed. At the workshop, the financial aid counselors told us how the information we provided went to the schools that we listed. Later, we would receive a form that included our Expected Family Contribution (EFC). From this, we would know how much my family would have to pay for college. I learned later that the financial aid that I received may not match that, but it did give an idea of what my education would cost my family. I felt so much pressure, hoping that number was as close to zero as possible.

Assistance with financial aid was not the only way that being a TRIO participant helped financially. Because many students in TRIO programs were economically disadvantaged, they were able to provide or direct us to fee waivers for standardized tests and application fees for colleges and universities. This helped my family a lot; otherwise, the costs of just applying to schools, which were $30-$50 per application, would have added up.

After high school graduation, I decided to attend SLU and the benefits of Upward Bound soon became apparent. All students, but especially FGS, must deal with academic and social integration in the university setting. This means that students must feel connected to their school's academic programs and content, along with a social connection to their institution (McKay and Estrella, 2008). During this integration, I did not go through the same adjustment issues that some other students encountered. I knew where buildings and classes were; living in the residence halls was enjoyable rather than stressful; being busy all the time was not unusual; I was academically prepared for my classes. In a way, I felt that college was easier than being in Upward Bound because I did not have to juggle high school plus classes on Saturday and had more flexibility and freedom. I could set up my schedule in ways that worked best for me, rather than following a schedule someone else predetermined. Instead of being intimidated about college, I felt prepared and relished the opportunity to stretch my wings.

NEW DIRECTIONS FOR TEACHING AND LEARNING • DOI: 10.1002/tl

Upward Bound allowed me to use an assertive accommodation strategy for success. Assertive accommodation strategy is when students use their first-generation status positively to achieve their academic goals (Orbe and Groscurth, 2004). By using programs specified for FGS, such as Upward Bound, Student Educational Support Services, and, eventually, McNair Scholars, this strategy enabled me to bond with other students based upon my status, especially other Upward Bound alumni. It was great having other students, who had similar experiences through TRIO, also working at being successful in college. It reinforced my belief that I could be successful, too.

Eventually I realized that I wanted to go to graduate school. This idea became more apparent my sophomore year, when SLU started a McNair Scholars program. The program, named after Dr. Ronald E. McNair who died in the *Challenger* explosion, offers career and academic advising, along with mentoring (Grimmett, Bliss, Davis, and Ray, 1998). The McNair program's goal is to get first-generation college and underrepresented students through graduate school and into academia. For several ethnic minority groups, there has been an increase in the number of doctorate degrees awarded. For example, the Survey of Earned Doctorates reports that 5 percent of African Americans received doctoral degrees in 1997. This number has increased to 7 percent in 2007 (National Opinion Research Center, 2007). As a college undergraduate student I knew that the McNair program could do for me what Upward Bound did. I would get training and preparation for graduate school and find out what was necessary for me to enter and succeed in graduate school. I was accepted into the McNair Scholars program during sophomore year.

The McNair program is structured differently from Upward Bound. Instead of taking classes every Saturday morning during the school year, there were seminars on aspects of applying to and succeeding in graduate school. These sessions covered topics such as what graduate schools were looking for in applicants, searching for graduate programs, writing personal statements, and adjusting to graduate school.

The McNair program has invaluable features. First, approximately ten students did summer research for eight weeks. In my research, which was entitled, "Call-Response as Cultural Performance: Verbal Interaction among African American Movie Audience Members," I used observations and interviews to examine how audience members used call and response in movie theaters. I know now how much this project helped me with long-term planning. That is, I was able to conceptualize a project, think about its ending, and work toward that end while dealing with the unexpected challenges that accompany research.

To complete our projects and prepare for graduate school, we were matched with a faculty mentor. Mentoring can help with socialization into academia and increase career satisfaction (Schrodt, Cawyer, and Sanders, 2003). My faculty mentor, Dr. Karla Scott, steadily guided me through my research and adjustment into graduate school and academia. This relationship developed past my initial summer work with her. I even call her my "academic mom" because her encouragement, nurturing, and pride in my accomplishments resemble that of my biological mother. Dr. Scott has always provided personal direction through my selection of graduate schools, support throughout my graduate programs, and assistance during the job application process.

Unlike Upward Bound, McNair Scholars was much less structured. That summer I conducted about forty hours of research per week. My time was spent between the library, computer lab, collecting data in movie theaters and with research participants, or with Dr. Scott. On Fridays, all the McNair scholars participated in workshops. This was the only time we would officially come together because we were doing our own research during the week. This developed independent learning in all of us because there was little direct supervision over us. In our workshops we discussed our research and had the McNair staff, faculty, and other graduate students talk with us about graduate school life, presenting at conferences, and finding funding for graduate school. This summer experience showed me how much I enjoy researching, learning, and creating new knowledge.

The next school year I attended the Heartland Research Conference in Kansas City, Missouri, and the National Research Conference in College Park, Maryland. At these conferences, I met other McNair scholars and faculty members at graduate programs, developed my curriculum vita with research, and gained conference experience. During the school year, I, along with the rest of the McNair scholars, presented my research to the SLU community.

An integral part of my success in McNair Scholars and, ultimately, graduate school was my relationships with Dr. Scott and the McNair Scholars staff. They corrected my assumption that applying to graduate school was just like applying to undergraduate programs. I believed you picked a school that had your potential major, and if my grades were as good as or better than others, I would get in. However, Dr. Scott and the McNair program administrators taught me that getting into graduate school not only involved emphasizing my assets, but also showing how I fit into the program. Dr. Scott also had me think long-term about what I wanted to research and study, and to find scholars I could work with. Even at conferences we attended together, Dr. Scott introduced me to other faculty members she knew in graduate programs and had me contact them for information, reviewed my personal statements, and helped me prepare for the conferences where I presented.

The McNair program enabled me to get through the graduate application process for my master's and doctorate degrees. I was taught which professors to approach for letters of recommendation (i.e., faculty who knew me well, not just faculty I received an "A" from in their class). I received feedback from my mentor and McNair staff on my personal statement. I was confident that I was able to put in strong applications to the schools.

Both Upward Bound and McNair Scholars equipped me well for my journey through higher education. Jehangir (2009) tells how FGS are able to use transformational learning, or taking knowledge and translating it into action. TRIO programs provided academic, social, and administrative knowledge that has shaped me to become an academic. Being an FGS, I did not know how education would change my career goals, and also influence me personally. I have found with TRIO programs I was given the resources, preparation, and support to succeed both professionally and personally for my academic pursuits.

References

Allensworth, E., Correa, M., and Ponisciak, S. *"From High School to the Future: ACT Preparation-Too Much, Too Late"* (Consortium on Chicago School Research Report). Chicago: University of Chicago, the Consortium on Chicago School Research, 2008. Retrieved June 1, 2011, from http://ccsr.uchicago.edu/publications/ACTReport08.pdf.

Coles, A. S. "Trio Achievers: The Promise of the Future." *Journal of Negro Education,* 1998, 67(4), 432–443.

Grimmett, M.A.S., Bliss, J. R., Davis, D. M., and Ray, L. "Assessing Federal TRIO McNair Program Participants' Expectations and Satisfaction with Project Services: A Preliminary Study." *Journal of Negro Education,* 1998, 67(4), 404–415.

Jehangir, R. R. "Cultivating Voice: First-Generation Students Seek Full Academic Citizenship in Multicultural Learning Communities." *Innovative Higher Education,* 2009, 34, 33–49.

McElroy, E. J., and Armesto, M. "TRIO and Upward Bound: History, Programs, and Issues—Past, Present, and Future." *Journal of Negro Education,* 1998, 67(4), 373–380.

McKay, V. C., and Estrella, J. "First-Generation Student Success: The Role of Faculty Interaction in Service Learning Courses." *Communication Education,* 2008, 57(3), 356–372.

National Opinion Research Center. *Survey of Earned Doctorates Fact Sheet.* Chicago: National Opinion Research Center, 2007. Retrieved June 1, 2011, from www.norc.org/NR/rdonlyres/B40E56EC-9A4F-4892-B871-E330BB689CD9/0/SEDFactSheet.pdf.

Orbe, M. P., and Groscurth, C. R. "A Co-Cultural Theoretical Analysis of Communicating on Campus and at Home: Exploring the Negotiation Strategies of First Generation College (FGC) Students." *Qualitative Research Reports in Communication,* 2004, 5, 41–47.

Schrodt, P., Cawyer, C. S., and Sanders, R. "An Examination of Academic Mentoring Behaviors and New Faculty Members' Satisfaction with the Socialization and Tenure and Promotion Processes." *Communication Education,* 2003, 52(1), 17–29.

LAKRESHA GRAHAM is an assistant professor of communication at Rockhurst University. Her research examines social class, namely in connection to race, gender, and intercultural communication. Her interests in studying FGS come from her experiences as a first-generation college student, along with studying social class and communication.

New Directions for Teaching and Learning • DOI: 10.1002/tl

SECTION TWO

First-Generation Students Join the Undergraduate Ranks

The authors extend the existing research about first-generation Native Americans at mainstream institutions by looking at Native Americans enrolled as first-generation college students (FGS) at tribal colleges. Using the results of interviews with faculty at tribal colleges, the authors discuss the challenges that first-generation college student Native-American students face, such as lack of family support and role models, lack of college preparation, and financial concerns.

Faculty Perceptions of the First-Generation Student Experience and Programs at Tribal Colleges

Jacqueline J. Schmidt, Yemi Akande

Although an increasing number of Native Americans are enrolling as first-generation college students (FGS) at postsecondary institutions, the percentage of those attaining bachelor's degrees or higher remains relatively low—11 percent, compared with more than 25 percent for the general population. Native Americans face not only the retention concerns of most FGS of family pressures, poverty, and a weak high-school education, but also must assimilate into a campus culture much different from their own (Hoover, 2004).

Tribal colleges were established in response to unmet higher education needs of Native Americans. They generally serve geographically isolated populations with no other means of accessing education at the postsecondary level (American Indian Higher Education Consortium, 2006). The mission of these colleges and universities is to not only provide education (as all institutions do), but also to foster campus cultures that preserve, enhance, and promote American Indian languages and traditions (Fogarty, 2007; Braun, 2008).

The 1998 report of the American Indian Higher Education Consortium found Native-American enrollment had increased more rapidly at tribal colleges than at mainstream institutions. From 1997 to 2002, student enrollment at tribal colleges grew by 32 percent compared to 16 percent growth in higher education overall (Williams, 2007).

NEW DIRECTIONS FOR TEACHING AND LEARNING, no. 127, Fall 2011 © Wiley Periodicals, Inc.
Published online in Wiley Online Library (wileyonlinelibrary.com) • DOI: 10.1002/tl.456

Previous research has focused on the experiences and programs of Native-American students and the role of Native-American faculty and staff in majority institutions (Fox, 2005; Shotton, 2007). However, the faculty perspective on the experience and programs for FGS at tribal colleges is an underresearched area, yet faculty involvement and commitment are vital to the successful running of these institutions. Furthermore, these institutions may provide valuable alternatives and insight on how to approach many of the problems typically faced by FGS.

This chapter provides a brief background on tribal colleges and presents the results of interviews with faculty from tribal colleges (many of them FGS themselves) on the challenges faced by FGS, their programs, and recommendations.

Tribal Colleges

The first tribal college was established in 1968. Fifteen schools were added in the 1970s, seven in the 1980s, seven in the 1990s; in 2005, there were thirty-five tribally controlled colleges and universities. They are located in thirteen different states, scattered across the West and Midwest (American Indian Higher Education Consortium, 2006). Today there are thirty-seven tribal colleges that are part of the American Indian Higher Education Consortium (Braun, 2008). Tribal colleges are accredited institutions offering 400 majors and 180 vocational certificate programs. Most are two-year institutions offering associate degrees. Nine offer bachelor's degrees and two offer master's degrees, but nearly all colleges offer four-year programs with other institutions through distance learning or transfer. They provide quality education in a variety of subjects, including technology, health care, and the liberal arts, while also serving as community centers, providing child care, and housing libraries.

Williams (2007) provides an excellent description of tribal colleges: A tribal college provides a "whole community" approach to lifelong education based on the principle that a student does not have to abandon culture or family to obtain an education. The average tribal college student is a twenty-seven-year-old single mother of three, and is often a first-generation student, making leaving home untenable and familial support necessary for success. Ninety-one percent of the American Indian College Fund's scholarship recipients are "nontraditional" students—they have dependents, are older than twenty-four years of age, and work full time—or have a combination of these characteristics.

Although many public tribal colleges and universities in the United States were established to serve members of a particular Indian tribe, in recent years their student population has extended beyond tribe members to students who are not members of any federally recognized tribe. Of thirty-two tribal colleges reporting for 2004–2005, 12 percent of students were non-Indian female and 6 percent non-Indian male (American Indian

Higher Education Consortium, 2006). Ashburn (2007) found that the institutions educate about 5,000 non-Indian students each year. Typical of these students is Dawn Stein, white, mother of one, thirty-three years old, works part-time, and wanted a college close to home. Although not a Native American, her stepmother is a member of a tribe.

Overall, tribal colleges serve an identity function for Native Americans. This cultural identity is critical as FGS social identity "served as a key motivator for success" (Orbe, 2008, p. 137).

Method

This chapter explores faculty perceptions of the FGS' experience at tribal colleges. Using a qualitative approach, in-depth, semistructured telephone interviews were conducted with twelve faculty members, one of whom was an administrator/faculty member. Interviews ran twenty to thirty minutes. The questions were open-ended in an attempt to get at the experience of faculty members teaching FGS at tribal colleges and their observations about how to work with their students. Following a phenomenological approach, these questions looked at the individual experiences, and, at the same time, provided an approach to develop some general meaning from the shared experiences. This research approach is similar to other studies with Native-American administrators (Murray, 2006) and other FGS (Cushman, 2007; Hand and Miller Payne, 2008).

Faculty members from fifteen random schools were solicited for interviews; faculty members from five schools were interviewed. The schools in the study are a good representation of tribal colleges. Three of the schools are in the Midwest and two in the West. Tribal colleges are located in the West and Midwest ranging from Michigan to Washington and south to Arizona and Texas. All of the schools offered associate degrees, two offered four-year degrees in addition to an associate degree, and one offered master's degrees. Three of the institutions were on a reservation and two were not. The populations of these schools ranged from less than 200 to more than 1,000 students. To protect privacy, the names of actual institutions and interviewees are not identified here.

The interview questions covered four basic areas: faculty perceptions of their college experiences, faculty perceptions of the challenges faced by current and former FGS, faculty perceptions of the value of special programs offered at their institution for these students, and suggestions for improvements in teaching FGS.

Questions asked were

1. If they had been a first-generation college student and, if so, what challenges they had faced.
2. Did they feel the experience of FGS had changed since they were in school? Explain.

NEW DIRECTIONS FOR TEACHING AND LEARNING • DOI: 10.1002/tl

3. What are the challenges faced by today's FGS? What are the challenges faced by Native-American FGS?
4. What percentage of their students do they believe are FGS?
5. What special programs, if any, does their school have for FGS? Describe these.
6. What has been the value of these programs? Explain.
7. What suggestions for improvement in reaching FGS do they have?
8. What suggestions for improvement in reaching first-generation Native-American students do they have?

All the questions were asked in each interview, but sometimes follow-up questions or clarifications were asked as faculty shared their own experiences as students and their interactions and observations of students. Of the faculty interviewed, 50 percent were female and 50 percent were male, 58 percent were first generation and 66 percent were Native Americans. Five faculty members came from one school, two each from three schools, and one from the remaining school. Their teaching experience ranged from five years to twenty-five years.

Findings

A number of challenges are faced by FGS.

Lack of Role Models and Family Support. Ninety percent of the faculty interviewed felt one challenge faced by first-generation Native Americans was a lack of "role models." This lack was demonstrated in several ways. First, many faculty members felt that Native-American students were unfamiliar with higher education's purpose. They lacked the knowledge of what to expect because they had not had other members of the family to tell them stories to make it "less mysterious." As one faculty member commented, "They (students) have no knowledge about what happens at college." Another professor related the story of a student who received his acceptance letter and thought it meant he had completed his degree. This lack of cultural capital or expectations of "how to do the student role" is similar to issues identified for Hispanic FGS (Harrell and Forney, 2003).

Second, faculty expressed a concern that the role models and experiences Native Americans did have might be negative. Several faculty members shared their stories of difficult assimilation. A Native-American male faculty member commented about having to ignore his culture when he attended school because "native language traditions were discouraged in public and Catholic schools." A female Native-American faculty member who had also attended public school stated that all her teachers were white and the classes such as history developed no connection to her culture or heritage. "There was a lot of ugly racism and the population was really separate," she said. Hopefully this situation has changed; however, current accounts of Native Americans indicate that there still is ignorance about Native-American culture and strong stereotypes on campus (Rolo, 2009).

Another reason for negative role models for Native Americans can be found by reviewing the history of their education. In the 1950s and 1960s, around 70 percent of Native-American children educated by the Bureau of Indian Affairs were sent to boarding schools (Robinson-Zanartu, 1996). Faculty members felt that family members, who had a bad "boarding" experience of their own, may assume their children will have the same negative cultural experience at college and discourage attendance.

Finally, community (place) is important in this culture. Given the lack of role models or bad models, leaving the community to go to college is difficult for many students. One faculty member stated, "For Native Americans there are few role models of people who are living away from the community, but are still part of the community." One female Native-American faculty member felt that a question many Native-American students face about going to college is, "Am I betraying my history and culture?" This was particularly true for students who attended a mainstream university.

Although Native-American FGS are similar to other first-generation groups such as Appalachians in the importance of wanting to remain close to family and community (place), the amount of support from family is very different. While studies show that Appalachian students (Hand and Miller Payne, 2008) and Mexican-American students (Prospero and Vohra-Gupta, 2007) felt their parents supported them, set educational standards, and were happy they were attending school, faculty interviewed in this study felt that because most Native-American parents did not understand the importance of college or had negative experiences, they were not supportive of the experience. One male Native-American faculty member said "they (parents and students) don't see the long-term goal—how what they are doing is preparing them to live, to get a job." Furthermore, faculty felt that parents/ family often need the student at home to help and see this role more important than attending college. This situation creates conflict for students. Of the top seven factors affecting retention, all of the twenty-three Tribal College Units (TCUs) reporting listed family obligations as a factor in retaining students (American Indian Higher Education Consortium, 2006).

Lack of Preparation. Seventy percent of the faculty interviewed felt a lack of preparation was a major challenge. One male first-generation Native-American faculty member commented that the "quality of education given on reservations is sub-par." The male first-generation Native-American administrator/faculty remarked, "We are getting students that are not sought after by big universities. A lot of our students have to take academic enrichment classes before they can enroll. Seventy-five percent of our students come from the area." Still another faculty member observed, "The issue is whether students come from the city or rural, and rural is the biggest problem." This concern is consistent with the AIMS report in which of the twenty-three TCUs responding, twelve listed lack of preparation as a factor in retention (American Indian Higher Education Consortium, 2006).

Faculty interviewed also identified low reading and math skills as a major factor why FGS in general do not succeed and related these low scores to cultural background for Native Americans. As one faculty member commented, "Their culture is an oral culture. There is not much reading material in the home . . . computer ownership is not the norm in many of their families." Historically, Native-American cultures have relied on an oral rather than written tradition of learning. For instance, traditional songs and stories are teaching methods. Robinson-Zanartu (1996) explains, "At one level they teach such building blocks of learning and things as sequence, cause/effect, and temporal orientation; at a deeper level they have holistic transcendence meant to teach deeper lessons concerning life" (p. 375). Writing as it is done in the traditional classroom focusing on the expression of one's thoughts, one faculty member commented, is not part of the cultural capital of these students. Other studies have found that Native-American students have trouble talking about themselves moving from a "we" based culture to a "me" based culture (Hoover, 2004).

These findings also relate to studies about Native-American learning styles. Native-American students according to Barber (2009) are mostly visual learners. Several authors indicate that learning in Native-American cultures is based on observation and demonstration. Students are taught by parents or elders "Watch, then do" (Morgan, 2009). Students do not display knowledge in the process of learning, but only when the student presents (Robinson-Zanartu, 1996). Additionally, their cultural thinking patterns are more relational, nonlinear, and holistic than cause-effect. An illustration of this holistic learning approach is evident in Tharp's description of a lesson plan devised by Yukon elders to teach the traditional craft of making moccasins of caribou skin (cited in Robinson-Zanartu, 1996, p. 378).

The sixteen-week unit began with preparations for the hunt; moccasins per se did not appear until the fifteenth week. To the elders' way of thinking, it is not possible to understand the moccasin outside the context of the leather, which is not understandable outside the spiritual relationship of the caribou to the land. Contrast this with the analytic way of proceeding in which we probably would have given the children the pattern to start cutting out the leather in the first fifteen minutes.

Still, other faculty members felt lack of preparation was "not that they don't have academic skills, they just don't have survival skills." Like other FGS, faculty mentioned students lacking both study and time management skills. Unlike other first-generation groups, however, faculty mentioned lack of knowledge of how to fit in or how to eat properly as types of these survival skills. One male Native-American, first-generation faculty member commented "eating right for the brain, students eat high fat, high carb and it affects the learning process. This is what I see for native students."

NEW DIRECTIONS FOR TEACHING AND LEARNING • DOI: 10.1002/tl

Another male Native-American faculty member remarked students needed to learn about substance abuse. Dr. Lindquist-Mala, president of Cankdeska Cikana Community College, agrees that tribal colleges have an obligation to engage the community in health issues, "Because we are the educators, we need to build community awareness about health with material that is culturally appropriate and understandable" (Ambler, 2007, p. 15).

Financial Concerns. Forty percent of the faculty interviewed listed financial reasons as a major challenge for FGS. Faculty members commented on the lack of resources and money for students. Of the twenty-three TCUs reporting as to the seven major factors affecting retention, twelve listed financial problems and twelve listed maintaining an off-campus job (American Indian Higher Education Consortium, 2006). This challenge is consistent for most first-generation groups.

Are These New Challenges? Among the faculty who had been FGS, most felt the challenges faced by today's students were very close to those they faced. Several still felt there was a difference in culture for current students. One Native-American man who attended college at a large university felt "it's a different world and competing with everyone is different. It is a little more cut-throat." The only change noted was in the amount of assimilation demanded and racism faced. One female Native-American faculty member felt today there was less racism, and that multiculturalism and diversity were more valued than when she attended college. Today classes especially at a tribal college build around tribal culture and history and adapt more to the community culture as can be seen in the nature of the tribal college and their programs described in the next section.

Programs for FGS at Tribal Colleges

When faculty and administrators were asked about special programs for FGS, most responded that they had no special programs for FGS at their school, but rather programs for all new students. However, faculty perceived that roughly 75–90 percent of their student population was first generation. Many faculty members felt that the tribal college attracted poorer students, both financially and academically, who would not be able to attend other colleges.

One of the main problems experienced by many FGS is the feeling of being the "outsider" (Cushman, 2007). The unique aspect of tribal college programs for first-generation Native Americans is their commitment to establishing community and cultural identity. As one faculty member whose school is on the reservation remarked, "If you are dealing with students from culturally diverse backgrounds, it is essential that they have a place where they have identity supported and have a support system of people who can help them. One of the things that helps with our students as far as college diversity is they are here at the reservation taking courses and don't have an identity issue."

NEW DIRECTIONS FOR TEACHING AND LEARNING • DOI: 10.1002/tl

Unlike programs at large universities with a variety of FGS, cultural identity is the foundation for most programs at tribal colleges. All the schools continue cultural traditions. Native language classes are offered at four of the five schools surveyed. Native artwork is displayed on the college campuses. Several faculty indicated that their institutions held powwows for students and offered programs for "re-traditionalizing students; letting them learn to dance in regalia and celebrate their history." One faculty member mentioned participation in the American Indian Higher Education Consortium Conference, a tribal college Olympics competition including racing, bow and arrow, hand drum, and traditional games.

Faculty at all schools indicated that they had counselors and tutors available to help with education. Programs differed in the amount of counseling and the degree of interaction. Even these standard support programs had a strong cultural orientation. Given the strong importance of community for this group, one faculty member indicated their school stressed student study groups not only to improve performance, but also to deal with identity and relationships, giving students role models and providing a small community for them. One school had recently started a series of programs designed to foster interaction with counselors. They assigned achievement coaches to students and developed a mentoring network of faculty and students to make counseling more individualized, thus emphasizing this culture's relationship component. One faculty member reported their school used traditional cultural type approaches to create community. Meals and talk often began or ended a class. During midterms and finals, they held "blue corn learning" sessions using traditional Native-American foods. Faculty at two schools indicated that class sizes were deliberately kept small (ten to twelve students) to allow for individual instruction and assistance. One other faculty member mentioned that one key to their success was small colleges, programs, and personalized service. "The smallness makes it work—you can't deal with sensitive issues in a bigger setting." Relationships are critical in this type of program and culture.

Several schools also developed special programs such as a first-year seminar dealing with what higher education is about, making it meaningful for students and giving it a context for their lives and giving them expectations and "empowering themselves to advocate for themselves." Others had an orientation program ranging from one week to several weeks aimed at making the transition to college easier. Most offered enrichment or remedial courses to improve student skill levels or study skills. These programs were offered in the summer before school or during the first semester. One school was using e-portfolios to identify learning goals for students.

Success of Programs. Many of these study and tutoring programs are in the early stages (first three years) at these schools and the results are not yet known. However, faculty commented on the positive differences already evident by using individualized counseling, cultural values, and setting expectations these programs have made.

NEW DIRECTIONS FOR TEACHING AND LEARNING • DOI: 10.1002/tl

Faculty at the various institutions felt the cultural programs were very successful in establishing identity and building community. This theme ran through several comments. One professor quoted his institution's president who, when asked the question, "What will a student see when they come to the campus?" responded, "They will see home." One Native-American first-generation female faculty member remarked, "Students come and see themselves, reflected in culture and studies, they can go elsewhere and not see themselves." Another female faculty member commented of her school, "There is a concerted effort to make it into a community that feels like home." A third female Native-American faculty member felt, "They know they are Indian; they want to get back in—they want to learn." Because most schools were located on the reservation, faculty felt this allowed the school and programs to be directly involved in the community.

Because many of the tribal colleges were two-year institutions, faculty believed that establishing this identity at the tribal college was critical in the first two years of school to develop a student's confidence to complete the four-year degree or advanced degree at a nontribal institution. This is consistent with a study that found Native-American students coming from a Navajo community tribal college had a retention rate of 88 percent, compared to students who did not come from tribal colleges and made up the bulk of the attrition rate of Native-American students (between 50 and 75 percent; Braithwaite, 1997).

The importance of cultural sensitivity was critical in courses, methods, and activities. Faculty/staff and former students who serve as role models are an important factor in Native-American first-generation success (Fox, 2005). One faculty member remarked that most of the staff at the institution had been students at the college. However, according to another faculty member, "It was not necessary to have ethnically similar faculty (to the students) as long as faculty have the knowledge of the culture and region and are committed so they can identify and communicate appropriately and have flexibility in addressing the cultural needs."

The value of these role models became evident as several told their own stories of why they had returned to teach at a tribal college as part of embracing their cultural heritage and community. When asked why he had chosen to teach at a tribal college, one male first-generation Native-American administrator said, "It was natural to come back, they needed me." One first-generation Native-American female faculty member said, "I waited for this all my teaching career, waited for an opportunity that has a stamp on it . . . to come back and reclaim this historic land where our students can succeed." Another female faculty first-generation Native American echoed this idea, "It was important to come back because it is important for native people and native reservations."

Faculty felt that not all students started or finished with the same level of cultural awareness and connection. Students who came from larger communities and cities had less initial cultural awareness. Awareness also differed by region of the country and tribe. However, faculty said they felt that for most students, once they were on campus, because "of the indigenous curriculum, students end up interested in their background and it strengthens their sense of identity." One female Native-American not first-generation faculty member said that "sometimes in the early years students don't want to stress identity, they vary in their sense of ties in the culture . . . however as they begin to mature and get comfortable you see increased expression and interest in the culture." Another related the story of a young woman who became empowered by reclaiming her cultural heritage. This success is consistent with studies that show that when Native-American students can take part in college support programs that emphasize Native-American language and cultural traditions, they are more likely to have college success (Hoover, 2004).

Suggestions for Future Programming. Several faculty interviewed felt there was a need to develop programs that allow students to gain cultural capital, develop role models, and broaden their experiences/perspective. One suggestion was to get former students to return to share their experiences, showing students more opportunities and providing more role models. Another faculty member suggested that students should spend a day or longer in a bigger setting (huge university) with more students to learn how important college is. "Maybe if they saw it in a bigger setting with more students . . . they would see how it affects them." Another suggestion was that programs be established with connections between the tribal colleges and four-year institutions during the students' time at the tribal college. This could be done in areas of research or projects, setting up teams from both institutions to work together.

One successful program in Ohio integrates college courses into the high school curriculum. Lorain County Community College offers an Early College High School program to motivate students who have the potential to be the first in their families to graduate from college. Students graduate with high school and associate degrees. These suggestions would also help ease the transition between the tribal college and four-year institution.

To improve student preparation, tribal colleges might follow the example of Fisk University, a historical black institution, in establishing summer programs for students. Students who participated were better prepared for class work and more engaged (Fischer, 2007).

Several faculty members suggested more programming to the Native-American community was needed to educate parents about the importance of a college education and the college experience and to build support for college attendance. Faculty felt that often pressure from family causes a student to withdraw. In this culture, family is critical. One suggestion, which was to take a group of students on a college road trip to visit their grandparents and parents, is modeled after early college education programs of historically black colleges and universities. This approach could educate the parents about the college experience, and perhaps reduce their need to hold on to the students. One school will begin this kind of program this fall. Another suggestion has been to use the concept of service learning for students to interact with the community (Rolo, 2009). In this way, the goals of the tribal college and education unite. Students receive academic credit and work with their community. Furthermore, members of the community can become more aware of what happens at the college and how education can enhance the lives of those in the community. A program that has worked well with Hispanic parents in generating support has been to hold a series of workshops for parents to find out what questions and concerns they have about colleges so they can be addressed (Fann, Jarksy, and McDonough, 2009).

Recommendations and Conclusions

Tribal colleges offer several lessons and alternatives for addressing the needs of FGS. This chapter provides a brief qualitative view of faculty perception of the FGS and success of programs at tribal colleges. Although research needs to continue, the following suggestions for faculty who work with FGS, particularly Native Americans, can be made.

- Personal relationships are critical. This is particularly true for oral cultures like Native Americans.
- Keep the programs and colleges small to build community and identity and encourage relationships. This refers to small classes, programs, and even colleges. Only five tribal colleges have populations of more than a thousand students. Seven have populations of 501–1000; eleven have 200–500 students; and nine have 200 or fewer students (American Indian Higher Education Consortium, 2006).
- Develop relationships with mainstream schools to provide bridges for students to go on for degrees or work/visit outside of the reservation.
- Provide programs for basic skill enrichment (math and reading) and run programs before students arrive on campus.
- Develop mentors to work with students. These mentors must be culturally sensitive and be able to communicate expectations about what to expect in college and how college work should be done. This difference in expectations is the "cultural capital" that traditional students have about the student role and is critical to success (Collier and Morgan, 2008).
- Encourage and support student study groups. Most Native American cultures are group/community based. For Native Americans and similar cultures, working together provides identity and reinforces cultural values.
- Develop courses to teach lifelong survival skills such as social skills and the relationship between health and learning, particularly for Native Americans and their communities.
- Appreciate and work within cultural life approaches. For Native Americans, this means respecting the oral, observational, holistic, and

reflective nature of Native Americans. Do not try to change students, but show them how to adapt and expand their skill sets.

- Build community, and tie cultural values into the program. Highlight cultural activities, holidays, and other events. This cultural tie develops identity and self-esteem. The culture of first-generation is too vague; find the uniting force such as Native Americans, mothers, Hispanics, etc. This is particularly important on larger campuses.
- Try alternative methods for research and education. Use more oral- and community-based experiences. For example, when studying this population we first tried to survey students and were unsuccessful. Faculty interviewed suggested that instead of written surveys, oral interviews would be more successful. Similar issues could be found with testing and other learning measures. Given the strong emphasis of community, service learning with application to community would be a good adaptation.
- Educate parents/grandparents of students on the importance of college and the college experience. Provide them with examples and role models of students who have completed college and still are part of their communities to provide a support group for the student at home.
- Develop outreach into tribal high school classrooms and the community to demystify the college experience.
- When appropriate, take the programs to the students (as in the example of placing the college on the reservation) or develop satellite programs rather than taking students from the community to the school. For Native Americans, this reduces financial and family obligations and provides role models within their community.

It is clear that FGS do share certain characteristics and needs, but that one program or approach will not fit the needs of all FGS. In approaching this larger group, awareness of individual needs and cultures should be encouraged.

References

Ambler, M. "Health and Education Go Hand in Hand." *Tribal College Journal*, 2007, *18*(4), 14–15.
American Indian Higher Education Consortium. *AIMS Fact Book 2005*. Norwood, Mass.: Systematic Research, 2006.
Ashburn, E. "Tribal Colleges Reach Beyond the Tribe." *Chronicle of Higher Education*, 2007, *53*(40), 20–21.
Barber, C. "Don't Know Much about Native American Students." *Teacher Librarian*, 2009, *36*(3), 2–6.
Braithwaite, C. A. "Helping Students from Tribal Colleges Succeed." *About Campus*, November-December 1997, 19–21.
Braun, J. "What's in a Name? Tribal Colleges Cultivate Students' Cultural Identity." *Tribal College Journal*, 2008, *19*(3), 14–19.
Collier, P., and Morgan, D. "Is That Paper Really Due Today? Differences in First-Generation and Traditional College Students' Understanding of Faculty Expectations." *Higher Education*, 2008, *55*, 425–446.

Cushman, K. "Facing the Culture Shock of College." *Educational Leadership*, 2007, 64(7), 45–47.

Fann, A., Jarsky, K., and McDonough, P. "Parent Involvement in the College Planning Process: A Case Study of P-20 Collaboration." *Journal of Hispanic Higher Education*, 2009, 8(4), 374–393.

Fischer, K. "A Historically Black College Takes a Hands-On Approach to Student Success." *Chronicle of Higher Education*, 2007, 53(29), A21–A24.

Fogarty, M. "Commitment to Building Prosperous Nations." *Tribal College Journal*, 2007, 18(3), 12–17.

Fox, M.J.T. "Voices from Within: Native American Faculty and Staff on Campus." In New Directions for Student Services, no. 109. San Francisco: Jossey-Bass, 2005.

Hand, C., and Miller Payne, E. "First-Generation College Students: A Study of Appalachian Student Success." *Journal for Developmental Education*, 2008, 32(1), 4–15.

Harrell, P., and Forney, W. "Ready or Not, Here We Come: Retaining Hispanic and First-Generation Students in Postsecondary Education." *Community College Journal of Research and Practice*, 2003, 27, 147–156.

Hoover, E. "For American Indians, the Keys to College." *Chronicle of Higher Education*, 2004, 50(46), 31–32.

Morgan, H. "Teaching Native American Students: What Every Teacher Should Know." *Multicultural Education*, Summer 2009, 16, 10–12.

Murray, S. "Wisconsin's Tribal Colleges Overcome Challenges to Enrich Their Communities." *Tribal College Journal*, 2006, 17(3), 28–32

Orbe, M. P. "Theorizing Multidimensional Identity Negotiation: Reflections on the Lived Experiences of First-Generation College Students." In New Directions for Child and Adolescent Development, no.120. San Francisco: Jossey-Bass, 2008.

Prospero, M., and Vohra-Gupta, S. "First-Generation College Students: Motivation, Integration, and Academic Achievement." *Community College Journal of Research and Practice*, 2007, 31(12), 963–975.

Robinson-Zanartu, C. "Serving Native American Children and Families: Considering Cultural Variables." *Language, Speech, and Hearing Services in Schools*, October 1996, 27, 373–384.

Rolo, M. A. "Native Identity and Community on Campus." *Diverse: Issues in Higher Education*, 2009, 26(9), 26–28.

Shotton, H. J. "Stories of Success: Experiences of American Indian Students in a Peer-Mentoring Retention Program." *Review of Higher Education*, 2007, 31(1), 81–107.

Williams, R. "Tribal Colleges: The Model for Cultural- and Community-Based Education Reform." *Diverse: Issues in Higher Education*, 2007, 24(21), 41–41.

JACQUELINE J. SCHMIDT is a professor of communication at John Carroll University in University Heights, Ohio. She was chair of the department from 1984 to 1999. She holds a Ph.D. and M.A. in communication from the University of Iowa. She earned a B.A. in communication with honors (Phi Beta Kappa) from Macalester College, St. Paul, Minnesota. Her research areas are diversity, first-generation/millennials, intercultural communication (Russia/Croatia), and organizational communication. Dr. Schmidt is a published author and has presented numerous papers at national and international conferences. She also consults for professional organizations and businesses.

YEMI AKANDE was born and raised in Nigeria. She moved to Missouri where she earned a bachelor's degree in speech communication from Southwest Baptist University. From there, she continued her academic career earning two master's degrees from the University of Oklahoma, one in human resources and organizational development, and the other in public relations and journalism. She later earned her doctorate in communications from the same institution. Dr. Akande worked several years in Chicago as the associate director of recruitment for the Institute for the International Education of Students (IES). She taught for four years in the Communication and Theatre Arts Department at John Carroll University. She is currently senior director for civic education at the Cleveland Leadership Center.

NEW DIRECTIONS FOR TEACHING AND LEARNING • DOI: 10.1002/tl

6

The authors use relational dialectics theory to argue that first-generation college students (FGS) often struggle with a give-and-take tension between getting involved in campus life and losing their familial and working-class identity. They suggest that because FGS straddle two different cultures of academia and home, institutions must address these tensions to improve the students' retention and graduate rates.

Understanding the First-Generation Student Experience in Higher Education Through a Relational Dialectic Perspective

Russell Lowery-Hart, George Pacheco Jr.

As colleges and universities face pressure to expand enrollments and provide access to diverse students, they find it difficult to recruit and retain first-generation college students (FGS; Crissman Ishler, 2005). First-generation college students are significantly less likely to graduate due to lack of family support, financial strains, poor academic preparation, and other barriers (Brooks-Terry, 1988; Orbe, 2004, 2008; Engle, Bermeo, and O'Brien, 2006). These obstacles make it difficult for FGS to transition into college and graduate.

Many institutions use support programs to improve FGS academic success. Unfortunately, these programs often isolate FGS, creating a protective group that does not fully integrate into campus culture. Education administrators recognize the responsibility to increase FGS populations, but the students often find that institutions do not meet their needs (Higbee, Lundell, and Arendale, 2005; Upcraft, Gardner, and Barefoot, 2005). Programs aiding FGS are often unpublicized or inaccessible to students. Many students argue that it is difficult to "fit in" because the programs create a separation between FGS and non-FGS (Wilson, 2000). The ostensible failure to "fit in" results in the student's incapacity for positive relationships with the college and for peer friendships.

Relational dialectics theory suggests that relationships are a give-and-take process in constant motion. For FGS, the give-and-take nature of their

NEW DIRECTIONS FOR TEACHING AND LEARNING, no. 127, Fall 2011 © Wiley Periodicals, Inc.
Published online in Wiley Online Library (wileyonlinelibrary.com) • DOI: 10.1002/tl.457

relationship struggles emerges from their desire to maintain cultural identity while navigating the college experience. First-generation college students enter academic settings with less knowledge about what to expect and are often at odds with familial expectations. The students' experiences reflect relational dialectic theory because they are situated in the margins, despite being in the same campuses and classes as their peers. Because relational dialectics highlight the tensions of any relationship, scholars now extend the dialectical perspective beyond the interpersonal dyad to other settings such as larger, social relationships in the college setting (Martin, Nakayama, and Flores, 2002; Orbe, 2008). Relational dialectical theory illuminates the relational and contradictory nature of intercultural communication. We believe our findings will help colleges develop more effective relationships with FGS.

Scholars propose that successful relationships are stable and able to manage change, struggles, tensions, and instability (Canary and Stafford, 1994). Relational dialectics theory explains how relationships are maintained despite tensions and instability. Relational contradictions, or dialectics, help define the relationship and actually keep it healthy.

Although researchers discuss many dialectics, in this chapter we focus on three dialectics: *integration–separation, stability–change,* and *expression–privacy* (Baxter, 1990). Each dialectic manifests both internally and externally. Integration–separation captures the basic tension between social integration and social division. Stability–change focuses on the opposition between continuity and discontinuity. Expression–privacy captures the oppositional tension between what is disclosed and not disclosed (Baxter, 1994). We explore the potential of these three dialectics below.

The FGS Experience

Altman (1993) asserts that dialectical tensions should be explored within an individual, which he termed intraindividual dialectical processes, and within groups, or intergroup dialectical processes with "parents and kin, friends, work associates, and the culture at large" (p. 28). Baxter's definitions (1990, 1994) can be extended. Internal manifestations are constituted within an individual's persona, and the culturally bound expectations that an individual feels constitute the relations dialectics.

External manifestations are constituted between a group and the larger, dominant culture in which an individual's group is embedded. Altman (1993) argues that intergroup cultural relationships involve the same dialectical processes occurring in other relational dyads. Our purpose here is to improve understanding of the "pushes and pulls" that FGS experience in campus culture. We pose the following questions:

RQ1: Do FGS experience internal intraindividual dialectical tensions within the collegiate setting? If so, how do students navigate them?

RQ2: Do FGS experience external intergroup dialectical tensions within the collegiate setting? If so, how do students navigate them?

Method

This interview-based study was conducted through the assistance of a University Success Academy program targeting FGS at a southwest, regional university. Four focus groups were conducted over eight weeks. We interviewed twelve FGS divided equally by gender. Several studies use similar sample sizes and techniques to investigate dialectics (Cissna, Cox, and Bochner, 1990; Rawlins, 1993; Sabourin and Stamp, 1995).

We used focus groups to create a climate for FGS to openly discuss issues about their experiences as minority students on campus (Schwitzer, Griffin, Ancis, and Thomas, 1999). The focus group sessions ranged from forty-six to sixty-eight minutes. The individual interviews ranged from nineteen to forty-two minutes. Open-ended interviews allow participants to expound on their experiences (Feldman, 1995). By analyzing the narratives, researchers can better understand the students' "lived reality."

The data was transcribed and formulated into inductive constructs. The constructs' validity was established through constant comparison (Silverman, 1995). This grounded theory method involves constructing relevant categories (Sabourin and Stamp, 1995), which in this study were integration–separation, stability–change, and expression–privacy dialectical tensions. Our method of data processing reflected the four stages identified by Lincoln and Guba (1985): (1) comparing incidents applicable to each other; (2) integrating categories and their properties, (3) delimiting the theory or construct, and (4) writing the theory or construct. After we completed the first three steps and identified emergent themes, we analyzed results in step four.

Results

Two intraindividual dialectical tension categories and two intergroup dialectical tension categories were derived from the focus group and interview transcripts. We examined each category through representative excerpts from the focus groups and individual interview transcripts.

Intraindividual Dialectical Tensions. Intraindividual dialectics highlight the internal forces representing the inherent contradictions between personal identity and the social expectations the individual feels. Intraindividual dialectics focus on a first-generation college student's internal tension. Two main dialectics ("in versus out" and "talking versus silence") emerged from the data.

In Versus Out. This term represents the battle between the students' desire to be seen as "in" the campus setting and the desire to remain "out" of collegiate culture. The dialectical pull occurred as the students struggled

NEW DIRECTIONS FOR TEACHING AND LEARNING • DOI: 10.1002/tl

to be proud of themselves and their roots versus the struggle to learn and adapt to the collegiate culture.

"Out" was defined as pride for noncollegiate roots and culture as embodied through self-identification and self-confidence. "Out" students don't see themselves as "college" students and struggle with avoiding that moniker. "In" was defined as the behaviors of the collegiate culture that FGS felt they must enact to survive in the culture.

"Out" epitomized FGS' fears and uncertainty about their survival in the campus setting. These students struggled to fit "in," knowing that doing so would help them succeed academically. However, they resisted fully embracing collegiate culture by remaining "out" to maintain their personal and social identity tied to their families and childhood communities. The following example from a female student illustrated the oppositions between "in" versus "out":

> "I walk to class in the morning and see people wearing preppy sweaters and holding their (Greek organization) pledge books and I wonder what makes them so confident. When I hang out with my family and friends from home I make fun of these same people. They seem to have it so easy. I don't feel like I belong, like I am a fraud. I want their confidence but I don't want to become them to get it, but I don't know how."

This student expressed the dialectical tension between the desire to fit "in" as a confident, comfortable student and the need to remain outside of the collegiate culture. Her family world makes fun of the people she wants to be like. This led to her fear of becoming like the other students because she may be rejected or "made fun of" by the people she loves. In the university setting, she saw herself as an uncertain woman needing to learn ways of being "in." Relational dialectics argue that people entering a relationship need to "fit in," whether that relationship is interpersonal or branches out into a group setting.

First-generation college students suggested that their ways of thinking and communicating conflict with the ways of thinking and communicating in the collegiate culture. The statement was made by a first-generation man:

> "I grew up in a small town—there were only fourteen in my class. Only three of us are in college . . . . We've known each other for all of school. Suddenly, I was in classes and the dorms with people that I didn't know. When they talk in the lobby, they're so happy and talk about how easy this teacher is or how stupid that teacher is. I wish I fit in with them because they aren't worried about school. But if I sat out there with them and talked like they do, it would be a lie . . . . I don't fit in with them. I don't even want to. I just wanna feel as relaxed about class as they do. To fit in, I felt like I couldn't be real and say how scared I was or how embarrassed I felt. It was like we grew up in different countries and spoke different languages."

NEW DIRECTIONS FOR TEACHING AND LEARNING • DOI: 10.1002/tl

The student's fear about failure placed him outside of the "in" group, whom he perceived as confident and comfortable in the collegiate setting. This "out placement" creates an internal struggle between the identity he already knows and the identity he wants to know. Fear of the unknown keeps him situated outside the "in group," which negatively affects his campus experiences. Another response illustrates how FGS handle "in" versus "out" tension: "I need a job to provide for my family. I come to class, do my work and go home. I don't have time for college. I hafta work, raise my kids. College aint for me. Some dude will be talking about a party or a magician that was on campus. That aint me. College aint me. I come here because I take care of my family."

This student not only demonstrated the struggle to understand his peers, but also the deep-seeded internal struggle of "having to" obtain an education. Many FGS' familial backgrounds do not emphasize education. They feel forced into a world they don't know or like to provide for the family. As a first-generation college student, he indicates that talks of parties and student activities are an "in" college culture and he does not fit in.

Negotiating their place in college forces FGS to minimize their interaction with peers, professors, and others. These students indicated that they go to class and then leave because they do not understand the "college" experience outside of class. Additionally, these students do not have peers to help them negotiate this dialectical tension. They seem to choose "out" because they do not understand how to fit "in." "Out" is a natural progression of the isolation many FGS experience. Roots, family identity, community identity, and lifelong friends are part of the dialectical pull these students face. Culture shock forces them into isolation. One student exemplified these feelings: "I am from the street and I know how to live there, I know the rules—who you talk to, when you talk to 'em, where you go and where you don't. These other people don't have to learn my rules, but I have to learn theirs."

As a result of the dialectic between "in" and "out," FGS had difficulty deciding to honor their own culture by ignoring the dominant one. They also struggled with learning and then adapting to the dominant culture. This tension forced students to question their own abilities as they worked to survive in a culture they fear they do not understand.

Talking Versus Silence. Whether in an academic or social setting, FGS struggled between being silent or talking with others, especially regarding their fears and uncertainty about the college experience. One student epitomized this dialectical pull while describing a speech class:

"We had to give an introduction speech where we talked about what made me who I am. The first two girls get up and give their speeches and one talks about how her parents made her take violin and study music as a kid and how it became her passion. The next one shows pictures of some country in Europe I'd never heard of and how the travel made her see the "possibilities"

NEW DIRECTIONS FOR TEACHING AND LEARNING • DOI: 10.1002/tl

of life. I thought, "I can't do this." I was gonna talk about how helping my dad fix cars at his shop taught me about hard work and taking care of my little brother and sister helped me grow up. In my house, if I said I was taking violin lessons I would have been laughed at . . . . I didn't tell them what really made me who I was. I talked about being in basketball and how it taught me teamwork. It was safe. I gotta B, and I was happy."

This student feared voicing her personal experiences because students in the "in group" would not understand, or, worse, make fun of her. The dialectical pull forced her to hide her identity because she feared being entrenched in the "out group."

The following discussion between two students further explains this internal tension. Specifically, these students addressed their reticence to discuss their families in social settings:

Student 1: "We are in this program together for first gen students and we live in the dorm where half of us are in this program, and the other side of the floor are just normal students. Well, our RA [resident assistant] kept trying to get us to all play ping pong in the lobby and have movie nights."

Student 2: "Yeah she wanted to show this movie about a talking pig, Babe or Baby, something, and told us it has good messages for being a college student."

Student 2: "This girl from the other side of the floor was cryin' 'cause the movie . . ."

Student 1: "She liked it, she liked that movie. Then the RA is asking us questions about what college things were we worried about. This other girl's roommate starts talking about how she hopes everyone will believe in themselves like that stupid pig did and that we can all do it. She's lookin at all of us from our side of the floor."

Student 2: "They wanted us to talk about how we could be that pig and started asking questions about our classes and families and boyfriends and I was . . ."

Student 1: "How am I gonna tell about my family to someone who cries over a talkin pig?"

Student 2: "Like, I thought it was nice they wanted to talk to us, but I didn't know if they would understand cause I didn't understand them."

Forced into silence, FGS are unable to take ownership of their education. They are visitors because the "in group" has structured the world in a language and set of experiences that the FGS don't understand.

These students suggested that they feel the tension of talking versus silence because they were afraid their experiences would not make sense to their peers. This lack of cultural connection heightened the dialectic and made them even more fearful to talk about their cultural identities. Notably, the tension between talking and silence was elevated when the topics of conversation were issues about college. One student said, "I'm in this class for freshmen where we talk about studying and time management. My teacher asked us to talk about our fears about college and write them on the board. I was afraid that the other students wouldn't have the same fears I did, that they'd laugh at me because I was afraid to leave my family and was scared about getting lost on campus."

Another student reflects this same talking versus silence tension with peers in her dorm room when talking with them about her family history and education attainment. She said:

"I don't 'look' like a first-generation student. I drive a nice car. My parents pay for my college. I don't even have to work. My friends assume I am like them, and I work to keep it that way. I was a cheerleader in high school; I was popular. I knew how to play the game. It is different in college though. You don't have cheerleading to make you fit in. So, when we were popping popcorn the first or second week of the semester, people started talking about their families, what they did, where they went to school . . . I'm not ashamed of my family. My parents have good jobs, but they didn't go to college. They are someone's boss. I didn't talk about them though."

Although this student was proud of her family, she faced the tension of whether to talk about them or remain silent. Her feeling of belonging to the "in group" outweighed her need to share her real identity.

Students did not perceive their concerns about college success as "normal" fears for the traditional college student. When FGS were asked to share personal information and concerns about college, they worried about others' perceptions and faced the dialectic of talking or remaining silent. Consequently, they remained silent.

Intergroup Dialectical Tensions. Intergroup dialectical tensions highlight the external forces that represent the inherent contradictions between the social values of the traditional college culture, ideologies of FGS culture, and the dominant collegiate culture. Two main dialectics (integration versus segregation and assistance versus resistance) between the FGS culture and the collegiate culture emerged from the data.

Integration Versus Segregation. As a group, FGS were conflicted as to when and how to infuse themselves into collegiate culture. Integration is the desire by FGS to be accepted and included in mainstream collegiate culture as a viable, worthy, and important group. Segregation is the desire for FGS to be a self-sustaining, separate group from others on campus. They felt tension between pressures to integrate in the college and to segregate from it. According to the following focus group of FGS, the dialectic of integration versus segregation is constant:

> Student 1: "I couldn't make it without the [first generation] program. It has given me a home. I feel comfortable around these people."

> Moderator: "Are you satisfied staying within just this group or do you see a time when you will not be a part of this group?"

> Student 2: "I will cling to you guys."

> Student 3: "But we can't take every class together like we are now, and we have different majors so we will not always have each other like we do now."

> Student 4: "I see posters for some student organizations, like fraternities and stuff, and I think about whether I could do it or not. I think it would be fun, but I don't understand the whole rush thing."

> Student 2: "I don't need to pay for friends."

> Student 4: "It's not paying for friends, it is being a college student, it's having fun. Don't you want that?"

> Student 3: "We all want to be a part of the university. I just don't know how . . ."

> Student 1: ". . . how to act. I am proud of my roots. But who I am doesn't fit in with who these other people are."

This conversation summarized the basic intergroup tension for FGS. They recognized their desire to integrate into the college, but are concerned about acting on it because that signifies steps toward leaving who they were. They feel safe with other FGS, but experienced tension with other students even though integration into campus culture might offer academic knowledge, potential employment, and scholarships or financial aid. As a group, FGS wanted to assimilate, but they expressed a need to protect themselves by segregating themselves—maintaining this marginal identity keeps them safe and linked to their familial identities.

A focus group discussion addressed these dialectical issues of integration versus segregation:

> Student 1: "The university has a lot of student organizations and the [program director] wants us to create an organization for first-generation students."

Student 2: "We already have our group, why do we need the university to make us write down who is president or treasurer?"

Student 3: "It would be fun to be able to do some of the things they showed us in orientation like the group singing competition and the trips but . . . ."

Student 4: ". . . but you have to do all of these things. Have you read the application that [program director] gave us? I didn't understand half of it. Who was the Robert Rule guy? We were supposed to get a bank account at the bank. It's a lot of work and it kinda makes me mad. Why does it have to be so hard just to be a student organization?"

Student 3: "You're right. I gotta know that stuff and it doesn't make sense to us, so we can be our own organization."

FGS indicated a need to segregate themselves as a group. As one participant stated, "I came here for a degree. I didn't come here to go to college." Through self-imposed segregation, they found support from each other while still expressing a need to integrate into university culture. In doing so, they perceived themselves as having greater opportunities but greater risk.

Assistance Versus Resistance. Similar to the intraindividual dialectic of "in" versus "out," FGS, as a group, experienced the dialectical tension of assistance versus resistance. The FGS wanted to be successful and knew using a university assistance program would help them. Conversely, FGS continually felt the dialectic pull to resist support programs because of fear or a need to be self-sufficient. One student described both his understanding for support programs and the resistance to them: "[Program director] keeps talking about using the tutoring for my math class. I know it would probably help, but at the same time, my family taught me that we don't accept help. We can take care of each other." This student saw a benefit from using assistance, but felt personal and familial pulls to resist using it.

The assistance versus resistance dialectical pull also resulted from fear. A focus group discussion illuminates this perspective:

Moderator: "This university created several programs targeting success of first-generation students. How do you feel about them?"

Student 1: "Well, I've used the online tutoring program because I don't have to talk to a person. I'm embarrassed that I don't get my math class. The people around me seem like they understand it. I feel stupid. I think tutors would see how dumb I am. But, that smart-thinking math stuff helps. They don't know me on there."

Student 2: "Sometimes all these programs make me feel even more insecure, like you have this group for first gens, you have this floor in the dorms for first gens, tutoring for first gens, special field trips for first gens, it's like we are so bad off that you have to do more for us that for other groups and it makes us stick out and tells everyone we are different."

Student 3: "But this group and our dorm and tutors help me. I like it. I feel safe, like someone understands."

Student 2: "Sure, but I don't like that the teacher and the tutors, who are the same age as us, look at us like we are so needy, like they are so good to help out the poor, dumb people."

Student 4: "We are dumb, we just differ . . ."

Student 1: "Different? Why are we different? Just because my mom didn't go to college I've gotta live in this dorm and take two classes with other people who are different? I like our group, but . . ."

Student 4: "Is that why you don't go to tutoring with us?"

Student 1: "Look around, it's not just me."

Student 5: "So if you weren't in this group, then you would go to tutoring? [Student name], you're full of shit."

The group understood the need for tutoring or other support services, but fear or discomfort about using them created their resistance to them.

One particular student identified another insight about the dialectical pull of assistance versus resistance. He said, "I sit in this history class and all these dates are confusing. So there is this study session before each test. I should go, but this stuff isn't gonna help me as an engineer. It doesn't affect my life. Why should I spend time on it?" Such examples reveal how FGS understand that assistance programs could improve academic success. The student resistance to these support initiatives reflects the exclusivity of who accesses them and the relevance of the course content to their lives.

Discussion

The two intraindividual dialectics and two intergroup dialectics help us understand the FGS experience in higher education. Understanding why FGS feel drawn to the "out group" will help educators and institutions retain these students.

When looking at RQ1, the data show that students do experience intraindividual dialectical tensions within the collegiate setting. The FGS' internal struggle represents two opposing views (melting pot or intensification of differences between cultures) on multiculturalism (Steele, 1995; Furr and Elling, 2002). In navigating these tensions, FGS are isolated because they fear losing personal identity. These fears steer them away from support programs, and away from relationships with students who are perceived as members of the "in group." For FGS to succeed in higher education, FGS must affirm the certainty of their cultural group. At the same time, if FGS want to academically succeed, they must stop focusing on their cultural identity as first generation.

The two views represented in the multicultural debate are apparent in the dialectical tension between in versus out and integration versus segregation. These students alternate between the oppositional poles of needing their identification with FGS as a culture and needing to be a part of the larger campus culture.

Most FGS understood their need to talk about their personal and social identities. However, their fear in talking about themselves creates a powerful dialectic. They constantly struggled with what, when, and with whom they could safely communicate. Their fears about communicating their college experiences were wrapped around larger fears of judgment from others. Because the FGS seemed to judge themselves as lacking important understanding of college, they assumed other people would have the same harsh judgments. Therefore, institutions must focus on creating trusting relationships with FGS.

Of all the dialectics, assistance versus resistance has the greatest implication for college response to FGS needs. Most colleges have support programs and offer resources targeting FGS. Although FGS understand the value of such services, tagging them as FGS only creates resistance from the group and hurts their self-confidence.

The dialectical tensions have further implications for colleges and universities. First, universities should make special efforts to include parents of FGS. The students in our study indicated that their parents had no understanding of universities and no desire to visit them. To combat this reality, universities may need to go to the communities instead of asking parents to come to campus.

Although Parent Day–type promotions are effective, these events are intimidating for the first-generation family. One student interviewed in this study indicated that her parents did not want to attend Parent's Day because they did not have an education. She said, "They thought everyone would be using big words, would be better dressed, and would make fun of them. They thought education was intimidating."

The dialectic of assistance versus resistance indicates that colleges face an uphill battle to convince students to access the resources needed to ensure academic success. The way services are marketed to students and the implementation of the resources may need to reflect the students' fears of being singled out as different.

Second, institutions should recognize the need for both in versus out and integration versus segregation dialectics. They can do this by creating programs emphasizing both sides of dialectical tensions. For example, schools could set up events that encourage the "in" and "integration" dialectical pulls, such as learning communities that integrate FGS with the "traditional" college student. Similarly, schools could set up joint programs designed to increase understanding between different student groups.

Third, institutions must offer instructional training for professors and graduate assistants about how to effectively develop relationships with FGS. Such training could teach instructors how to include diverse student populations into the class, address the dialectical tensions, and create safe learning environments for FGS. New faculty and staff orientations could include such training for FGS issues.

Fourth, FGS perceive that support programs also isolate and shine an uncomfortable spotlight on them. Institutions should reevaluate their programs in a way that addresses the dialectics discussed in this study.

Institutions of higher education face an important challenge. They must admit that their relationships with FGS are troubled, and then they must honestly and heartily attempt to develop and maintain such relationships. It will not be an easy process, but it is a necessary one.

References

Altman, I. "Dialectics, Physical Environments, and Personal Relationships." *Communication Monographs*, 1993, *60*, 26–34.

Baxter, L. "Dialectical Contradiction in Relationship Development." *Journal of Social and Personal Relationships*, 1990, *7*, 69–88.

Baxter, L. "A Dialectical Approach to Relational Maintenance." In D. Canary and L. Stafford (eds.), *Communication and Relational Maintenance*. New York: Academic Press, 1994.

Brooks-Terry, M. "Tracing the Disadvantages of First-Generation College Students: An Application of Sussman's Option Sequence Model." In S.K. Steinmetz (ed.), *Family Support Systems Across the Life Span*. New York: Flenum Press, 1988.

Canary, D., and Stafford, L. *Communication and Relational Maintenance*. New York: Academic Press, 1994.

Cissna, K. N., Cox, D. E., and Bochner, A. P. "The Dialectic of Marital and Parental Relationships within the Family." *Communication Monographs*, 1990, *57*, 44–61.

Crissman Ishler, J. L. "Today's First-Year Student." In L. Upcraft, J. Gardner, and B. Barefoot (eds.), *Challenging and Supporting the First-Year Student*. San Francisco: Jossey-Bass, 2005.

Engle, J., Bermeo, A., and O'Brien, C. *Straight from the Source: What Works for First-Generation College Students*. Washington, D.C.: Pell Institute for the Study of Opportunity in Higher Education, 2006.

Feldman, M. *Strategies for Interpreting Qualitative Data*. Thousand Oaks, Calif.: Sage, 1995.

Furr, S., and Elling, T. "African-American Students in Predominantly White University: Factors Associated with Retention." *College Student Journal*, 2002, *36*, 188–202.

Higbee, J., Lundell, D., and Arendall, D. *The General College Vision*. Minneapolis: General College Center for Research on Developmental Education & Urban Literacy, 2005.

Lincoln, Y., and Guba, E. *Naturalistic Inquiry*. Newbury Park, Calif: Sage, 1985.

Martin, J., Nakayama, T., and Flores, L. "A Dialectical Approach to Intercultural Communication." In J. Martin, T. Nakayama, and L. Flores (eds.), *Readings in Intercultural Communication: Experiences and Contexts*. Boston: McGraw-Hill, 2002.

Orbe, M.P. "Negotiating Multiple Identities Within Multiple Frames: An Analysis of First-Generation College Students." *Communication Education*, 2004, *53*, 131–149.

Orbe, M. P. "Theorizing Multidimensional Identity Negotiation." In M. Azmitia, M. Syed, and K. Radmacher (eds.), *The Intersections of Personal and Social Identities*. New Directions for Child and Adolescent Development, no. 120. San Francisco: Jossey-Bass, 2008.

Rawlins, W. K. *Friendship Matters: Communication, Dialectics, and the Life Course*. Hawthorne, N.Y.: Aldine de Gruyter, 1993.

Sabourin, T. C., and Stamp, G. H. "Communication and the Experience of Dialectical Tensions in Family Life: An Examination of Abusive and Nonabusive Families." *Communication Monographs*, 1995, *62*, 213–242.

Schwitzer, A., Griffin, O., Ancis, J., and Thomas, C. "Social Adjustment of African American College Students." *Journal of Counseling and Development*, 1999, *77*(2), 189–197.

Silverman, D. *Interpreting Qualitative Data: Methods for Analyzing Talk, Text, and Interaction*. London: Sage, 1995.

Steele, S. "The Recoloring of Campus Life: Student Racism, Academic Pluralism, and the End of a Dream." In J. Arthur and A. Shapiro (eds.), *Campus Wars: Multiculturalism and the Politics of Difference*. Boulder, Colo.: Westview Press, 1995.

Upcraft, L., Gardner, J., and Barefoot, B. *Challenging and Supporting the First-Year Student*. San Francisco: Jossey-Bass, 2005.

Wilson, M. "Reversing the Plight of African American Male College Students." *Black Issues in Higher Education*, 2000, *17*(18), 175.

RUSSELL LOWERY-HART *is vice president of academic affairs of Amarillo College. Before assuming the role of VP at Amarillo College, he was associate vice president of academic affairs and professor of communication at West Texas A&M University. He was responsible for the creation, implementation, and assessment of WTAMU's Quality Enhancement Plan (QEP), Engaging the First Year Student, and developed ten initiatives designed to engage students and faculty through a reformed core curriculum experience. Dr. Lowery-Hart's publications and conference presentations focus on underrepresented student population successes in higher education. Dr. Lowery-Hart earned his Bachelor of Science degree in speech communication from West Texas A&M University, master's degree in communication studies from Texas Tech University, and Doctor of Philosophy in gender and diversity communication from Ohio University. Before returning to WTAMU, Dr. Lowery-Hart was an assistant professor of communication studies at St. Edward's University in Austin.*

NEW DIRECTIONS FOR TEACHING AND LEARNING • DOI: 10.1002/tl

GEORGE PACHECO JR. is a first-generation college student and an assistant professor of communication at Angelo State University. He joined the Department of Communication, Drama and Journalism's full-time faculty in 2008 after completing a Ph.D. in communication studies at The University of Southern Mississippi. His dissertation analyzed Hispanic/Latino comedians' use of jokes to rhetorically influence audiences' beliefs about culture and ethnic stereotypes. Dr. Pacheco earned bachelor's and master's degrees at West Texas A&M University. His research interests focus on the use of humor as a rhetorical device, Hispanic/Latino stereotypes/cultural identities, and first-generation studies. Dr. Pacheco is a member of the National Communication Association, Southern States Communication Association and the Texas State Communication Association.

The authors found that the experience of academic dismissal for first-generation college students (FGS) differs from that of non-FGS in that the FGS cited wrong course choices, inability to examine personal strengths and weaknesses, and not seeking academic help as reasons for dismissal. FGS who appealed the institution's dismissal decision indicated that if permitted to re-enroll, they would become more involved in campus and seek faculty contact; these behaviors, the authors suggest, are crucial for the students' academic success.

First-Generation Issues: Learning Outcomes of the Dismissal Testimonial for Academically Dismissed Students in the Arts & Sciences

Jennifer Brost, Kelly Payne

Academic dismissal resulting from poor scholastic achievement is an unfortunate reality at American universities, and one that involves students, faculty, and academic advisers. This chapter analyzes learning outcomes of the academic dismissal process for first-generation college students (FGS) resulting from a year-long study conducted at a midwestern research university. Although this study's data are particular to this university, the research addresses widespread first-generation issues. Higher education institutions generally establish academic standards such as dismissal processes to ensure that students progress in due time toward graduation. Universities also need to verify that students receiving federal aid are making "reasonable academic progress" according to current federal financial aid standards. As a result, students whose grades fall below passing, indicated by a C letter grade at most institutions, are placed on academic probation. If students continue under probationary status, the university may consider academically dismissing them. Once dismissed, students generally have three options: appeal for immediate reinstatement, take "time out" while working on courses at a community college or online and then appeal for readmission, or leave the university altogether without appealing.

This study deals only with students who appealed for reinstatement. These students are required to meet with an academic adviser to discuss

New Directions for Teaching and Learning, no. 127, Fall 2011 © Wiley Periodicals, Inc.
Published online in Wiley Online Library (wileyonlinelibrary.com) • DOI: 10.1002/tl.458

their academic success plans and complete the requisite appeal forms, including a written testimonial statement. It is the advisers' responsibility to encourage an open dialogue about the reasons for dismissal and the individual student's educational aspirations. In addition, the dismissed student must submit documentation supporting his or her readiness to return to the university. Such documentation could include letters of support or explanation from professors, grade changes, and proof of situations that triggered the subpar academic performance but which have since been remedied, or evidence explaining extenuating or aberrant circumstances. In the dismissal testimonial, students at the university under consideration are required to submit one typed page addressing why they were dismissed and how they expect to succeed.

With this process in mind, the research questions that guided this work are: (1) Do FGS make up a significant percentage of academically dismissed students? (2) What factors lead to FGS' dismissals? And (3) What are the educational gains of requiring FGS to go through a written appeal process to be eligible to return to the university? Answers come from contrasting sixteen undergraduate students' surveys, focusing on how the responses of FGS compare to their non-first-generation peers.

Kuh's (1994) "learning outcome clusters" is helpful in providing an articulation of learning behaviors that dismissed students need to develop. Kuh's learning outcome clusters was used as a rubric for the kind of learning that one hopes FGS will make of their university experience. The five learning outcome clusters defined by Kuh are cognitive complexity, interpersonal and intrapersonal competence, practical competence, knowledge acquisition and application, and humanitarianism. Of the five outcomes, three most germane to the study of academically dismissed FGS are cognitive complexity, interpersonal and intrapersonal competency, and practical competency.

Kuh's (1994) research focuses on links between out-of-class experiences and desired student learning outcomes. Cognitive complexity includes skills such as: reflective thought, critical thinking, quantitative reasoning, and intellectual flexibility (Kuh, 1994). One learning outcome from the cognitive complexity learning outcome cluster may be measured by "[Students' ability to] articulate the pro's and con's about a complex issue and formulate their own position regarding that issue" (Keeling, 2006, p. 22).

Interpersonal and intrapersonal competence skills include a coherent, integrated constellation of personal attributes (e.g., identity, self-esteem, confidence, integrity, appreciation for aesthetic and spiritual qualities of life and the natural world, sense of civic responsibility), and working with people different from oneself (Kuh, 1994). Keeling (2006) adds to the skill set, "personal goal setting, meaningful relationships, interdependence, and collaboration. Students will be able to describe their skills and interests and make appropriate choices of major and early career" (p. 24).

NEW DIRECTIONS FOR TEACHING AND LEARNING • DOI: 10.1002/tl

The practical competence learning outcome cluster includes skills that reflect an enhanced capacity to manage one's personal affairs (e.g., time management, decision making, economically self-sufficient, and to be vocationally competent; Kuh, 1994).

Method

The participants in this study were undergraduate students who were academically dismissed during one of three terms: fall 2007, spring 2008, or summer 2008. The researchers telephoned these students or administered the survey during advising appointments. Consent was voluntary. The sample consisted of six women and ten men. The mean age of the sample was 20.75 years. There were three freshmen, five sophomores, three juniors, and five seniors. Of the sixteen students surveyed, seven were FGS (43.8 percent), and four students elected not to respond to the first-generation question, but could have fit the definition of a first-generation college student.

The instrument used in this qualitative study was a self-assessment survey. The survey questions were grouped together by learning outcome cluster: cognitive complexity, interpersonal and intrapersonal competence, and practical competency. The researchers created questions with the assumption that answers would fall into the three learning outcomes clusters. For example, questions in the cognitive complexity cluster asked the students to engage in reflective thinking and gauge their perception of their academic difficulties. Additionally, interpersonal and intrapersonal competence cluster questions addressed factors that led to dismissal, abilities to succeed academically, and support needed to be successful. Last, the practical competence cluster asked the students to speak about campus resources they intended to use, how they manage their priorities, and what steps they plan to take to avoid academic dismissal in the future. At the end of the survey, the students could provide additional remarks if they desired. The study was designed to measure how learning outcomes of FGS differ from that of non-FGS.

Results

The results are categorized according to cognitive complexity, interpersonal and intrapersonal, and practical competence.

Cognitive Complexity. When FGS were asked "What have you learned about yourself from the dismissal process?" they overwhelmingly discussed the opportunity for a second chance. One student reflected on his major choice, "[I learned that it is] better to do what you are good at (English and communication), not what you think you should do (exercise science)." This response emphasizes the discrepancy between an ideal major and the challenge in completing the actual curriculum. This first-generation college student directly connects choosing the wrong major with his underperformance and, significantly, does not shift the blame beyond himself. Another first-generation college student stated, "[I] learned I am overly optimistic . . . I was always hoping . . . [that] maybe my situation was enough to be able to at least get another chance." Again, a discrepancy appears between the desired and the actual outcome, which suggests an inability to effectively weigh one's strengths and weaknesses. While still another first-generation student said, "[I] am better prepared now to achieve goals that I want to do academically . . . [I] made a mistake when I was in school . . . [By] not getting help when I needed it."

Non-FGS' responses differed slightly from first-generation responses. They showed more disconnect between the development of critical thinking and the student learning outcome. One student stated, "I don't have enough self-accountability. I rely on assumptions and statements made by others too much." Independent thought as well as self-advocacy are absent from this first response; however, the student is claiming responsibility for the consequence. Not all students were successful in self-assessing their learning. For instance, one student claimed, "[I] did not learn anything . . . . [I was] dismissed because of grades but that was due to sickness, not because of performance." Although illness sometimes plays a role in dismissal cases, it is seldom the only factor.

Next, students were asked, "Describe the advantage and/or disadvantage of being required to write an appeal statement about your academic difficulties." The first-generation respondents highlighted the advantages of writing the dismissal statement as a reflective and healing process. "It makes you really review what you did wrong to place yourself in that position," noted one student. "Writing [the] statement helped me see what I did wrong and what I need to do to get better," said another student. One particular first-generation student found writing his statement "advantageous." This student said writing the appeal "gave him a different perspective . . . mainly [about] his career and further education. By reflecting on his academic difficulty, he realized he was "wasting too much time." Writing is a crucial academic skill, but based on these responses, it also seems to offer students an opportunity to think more critically about their choices.

Non-FGS' responses focused on the writing requirement of the dismissal appeal. As one student noted, "[I am] good at writing . . . [and] expressing myself . . . [I] liked that it was a written process." Another added, "It is good that one can reflect on the performance and analyze." However, some students found difficulty in writing their statement, "[The disadvantage is that I] cannot show emotion . . . [and I] could not express myself fully . . . [I] would rather have spoken to someone face to face . . . [my] situation was not easy to explain on a one page essay." Unlike their first-generation peers, these students focus on their strengths and move toward a critique of the process rather than themselves.

The third and final question asked, "How did writing the appeal statement affect your perception of your academic difficulties?" FGS communicated that the statement helped them reflect on their performance. "It took me a while to write because it made me think about absolutely everything I had done wrong . . . [the act of writing the appeal statement] made me think I could have done better," said one first-generation student. Another noted, "Writing the statement made me think differently about academic difficulties . . . [it] opened my eyes and made me see how I could improve." In this last case, writing is explained as a revelatory process, and one that allowed the student to see a path toward improvement of academic behavior.

Similarly, non-FGS echoed the same sentiments as their first-generation peers that the statement helped them reflect on their performance. Time management, personal responsibility, the balance of academic responsibilities, and students' life beyond the classroom were apparent in all student responses to this question.

Interpersonal and Intrapersonal. The first interpersonal and intrapersonal question asked of students was, "What factor(s) had the greatest impact on your academic dismissal?" FGS noted time management and rigor issues as the most common factor in their dismissal including "attendance," "trying to deal with math and science courses," "material was hard to understand," "time allocation," and "procrastination and laziness."

On the other hand non-FGS listed factors, including "took on too much too fast," "I was basically screwing off," "the marijuana, choosing to stay out late and sleep through classes," "I had less loans so I had to work extra hours," and "free reign and being by myself for the first time." Non-FGS seem to note answers that were rooted in responsibility and transitions from adolescent to adulthood, whereas time management and academic rigors were mentioned more frequently by FGS.

When students were asked, "Consider what you wrote in your appeal statement. How would you describe your ability to succeed academically?" Most FGS and non-FGS cited that they feel like they have what it takes to succeed academically, but other factors stand in their way. One first-generation student claimed, "[I have a] much better chance of succeeding now . . . [I am] confident in the schedule I have now." Note the factor that time plays in this student's idea of what may be accomplished. Now, he or she can succeed, but for some reason prior to dismissal, success was not possible. "[Academic abilities] are strong as long as I make better use of my time," says a student. Another student states, "I am capable of performing at an ultra elite level . . . [but] I cannot fully concentrate on school . . . I am capable of earning superior marks if academics are a priority." Here, note the "if." If academics are a priority then the student can earn passing grades. For some dismissed students, college pressures are not the priority. Another student echoes this sentiment, "[My ability is] strong as long as I make better use of my time." One student states her mental health issues as a hindrance to her performance, "I was a . . . National Merit scholar . . . I'm wonderful at academic success, but not when I can't even get out of bed and no one [cares]." These responses attest to a discrepancy between students' perceived ability and the consequence of underperformance, as outside factors are implicitly blamed for dismissal.

That both first-generation and non-first generation dismissed students discussed their competence and ability suggests that one's previous family experience at university is not necessarily the only factor at stake. Rather, it seems that the mindset of dismissed students is one of academic confidence.

The third, and final interpersonal and intrapersonal competence question asked was, "What kind of support do you need to be academically successful?" All students stated that relationships with advising center and faculty needed to be stronger. One student stated, "[I] would like to have a better relationship with faculty." Another said, "Good relationships with professors and TA's [are important] . . . [need to] be comfortable talking to them." Another student said, "Advisers are helpful in making things clear." Clearly, students view advisers and faculty as key resources. It is important to note that non-FGS did not admit to using these resources as often as FGS. Students also mentioned that family and friends played a significant role. One non-first-generation student stated, "Friends are very important . . . my mom helps with every problem I ever had with college." This statement is important because FGS, who do not have parents that understand the collegiate experience, did not cite family as much as non-FGS. One first-generation student noted what that student needed from family and friends were "encouraging words."

Practical Competence. The first practical competence question asked was, "What campus resources do you plan to use in the future?" All students spoke of institutional support in terms of their needs. "I need self-realization and pushing from advisers . . . [I] need to see advisers about where I stand," said one student. "[I need a] better relationship with teachers and advisers," said another student. One first-generation student spoke of the need of institutional support and lack of familial support: "during the school year [I need] faculty . . . [I have] RA and intimate [relationship] support . . . [I] had [a] good relationship with [my] RA . . . [however] as far as family goes, [I] was not encouraged to go to college."

Like the previous question, most students noted that they would use advising. An equally important concern is why students had not sought out or explored such resources before, but none of the responses addressed this issue. Campus resources such as math resource center, library, Upward Bound and TRIO programs, and student involvement were also mentioned. All FGS cited advising as a resource they would use. It is important to note that both non-first generation and first-generation students articulated the value of campus educational resources, although they admitted to not having sought out such resources.

Second, students were asked, "How do you manage your priorities?" FGS stated that they attempted to put academics first. "Right now my priority is a letter grade . . . classes come first . . . I study before I work or play or [do] anything outside of class," said one student. Another said,

"Academics is now my number one priority over employment." However, other FGS noted their struggles in putting academics first, "Employment, family is how I manage [my priorities] . . . I try to strive and put academics first, but unfortunately [that] was not the case." This response demonstrates the understanding of the difference between one's attempt to prioritize and the outcome of dismissal.

Most non-FGS listed academics as their first priority, "School, then family, God, friends, work," noted one student. One student elaborated, "Based on severity I normally put school first, work second, relationship with my girlfriend third . . . I give my family zero attention unless there is an emergency."

The third and final practical competence question asked, "Based on your written appeal statement, what steps do you plan to take to avoid academic dismissal in the future?" FGS cited changing their study habits. In contrast to their non-first generation peers, they focused more heavily on their future plans, as if there was no question on whether student learning behavior would change. One student responded, "[I] plan to study every day at least three or four hours, ask questions in class, participate more, and study more in advance." Another added, "I will just buckle down and study more." Another student speaks about advising, "[I will] work fewer hours and spend more time on campus in advising."

Non-FGS focused more on the present and stated that they needed to change their study habits and time management skills. One student noted, "Do all class assignments when I get back from class, not later . . . schedule work around classes, [whereas I] used to schedule class around work times." Another stated, "Work [in classes] harder and work less hours . . . I will need to take out more loans." One student noted he needed to change his social surroundings, "drugs are not the right answer. I need to be involved with different people . . . focus like [I] used to in high school." In these responses, pressures beyond the classroom become evident, as students addressed employment obligations and peer pressure as contributing causes of underperformance.

After the self-assessment was complete, students could add additional comments. Only two FGS chose to comment further on their experiences. One stated, "I think that the people involved were very fair and helpful . . . at first they wanted me to take a semester off and go to community college . . . my ambitions are too high for that." The second student said, "The support and procedures have been very positive, [I] would like to see that if a kid is struggling, the adviser should call and follow up . . . make student come in for appointment . . . there was nobody from the university [to turn to] . . . [I] had to be proactive about it." These responses are telling because both students indicate that the process seemed "fair," but that they felt more comprehensive advising should have been required. The responses suggest that FGS would have benefited from a process in which

NEW DIRECTIONS FOR TEACHING AND LEARNING • DOI: 10.1002/tl

advising was mandatory, but both students failed to account for the reasons why they did not seek out resources.

Findings

In the interviews, FGS reported that the written dismissal process helped them confront and reflect on their academic difficulties as well as those circumstances beyond academics that affected their successful completion of college courses. As a result of completing the dismissal process, students reported higher levels of cognitive engagement, interpersonal awareness, greater interest in becoming competent in practical skills, and greater interest in being more engaged upon returning to the university.

FGS reported the benefits of reflective thought, connecting academic progress or grades to their behavior and attendance. However, there were some instances wherein FGS spoke of self-efficacy, but then followed up with a statement excusing their behavior. This suggests that the learning outcome gains are ongoing, and that students would benefit from repeated reflective exercises. Additionally, students expressed the genuine intention to get more involved on campus and work less. Students commented frequently on importance of student involvement and engagement with faculty and advisers. This point seems crucial to student success. Indeed, the more faculty contact and opportunities students have to interact with their educational instructors, the more they are apt to feel their work matters. The inducement to complete assignments seems directly related to whether students think that a faculty member will notice. The researchers also noted that students' interpersonal and intrapersonal relationships prior to dismissal were not necessarily supportive. For instance, some first-generation responses indicated the negative effect of peer pressure or unsupportive family.

The researchers expected FGS to comment on the benefit of deep reflection in relation to their cognitive development. What the researchers learned was that cognitive development is an ongoing process, resulting in some students reverting to past behaviors like transferring blame.

For the intrapersonal and interpersonal competencies, the researchers expected FGS would assert the importance of university resources and on-campus student engagement, and they did. The researchers also hoped that FGS would address whether or not they exploited these resources before and whether they had a previous understanding as to the extent of the resource offerings, but students did not include information in their responses. Overall, the survey responses showed inconsistencies between FGS' self-perception, especially in the number of responses that assumed an inherent ability to succeed and the skill level required to attain educational goals. Second, FGS and their non-first generation peers showed similar reactions to the dismissal process, except that FGS did not emphasize the role of parents in their academic success. Also, FGS did not explicitly address their first-generation status, indicating that their first-generation identity is not perceived as an overriding factor of their success.

Last, in practical competency, the researchers expected students to admit struggling with life in and outside class, including expression of specific practical skills such as time management and prioritization of responsibility. FGS did so consistently, but they did not always address how they would achieve these competencies. It should be noted that FGS seemed to be aware of how crucial practical competency is to their academic success. However, they also noted that they need additional support from faculty, family, and advisers to realize this competency. At institutions where students must seek out resources, the burden of finding support rests on students who have not demonstrated a competence of how the university works. As a result, the researchers found that small gains in practical competency are crucial for dismissed students. Moreover, time management and decision making were emphasized by FGS as key factors in avoiding future probation or dismissal.

Applications for Faculty and Staff

Overall, students reported higher levels of cognitive engagement, interpersonal awareness, competency in practical skills, and more engagement upon returning to the university. This suggests that student underperformance could be helped through promotion of these skills earlier on. To cultivate these skills, faculty and university staff who work with FGS should implement strategies that promote critical thinking, advising, and mentoring.

The difficulty lies in identifying FGS, especially for faculty teaching large class sections. Therefore, the researchers recommend faculty ask their students-at-risk, i.e., those who are underperforming, to attend office hours or make an individual appointment. There, the faculty member could ask the student about their academic background, whether they have siblings or parents who have gone to college who might provide more support. Moreover, faculty members should find out what first-generation campus resources exist and refer students to them. Other strategies may include frequent e-mails asking students to come in to discuss class activities or performance with faculty/adviser, self-assessment documents for students to reflect on their academic difficulties (ideally this document would be completed prior to the faculty/adviser meeting), monitor students on probation and dismissal (including after students get off probation), provide planning guides and/or show students how to use them, and ask students on probation to provide midterm reports from instructors. Targeting probationary students, not just dismissal students, could also help identify students-at-risk early on and perhaps prevent future dismissals.

NEW DIRECTIONS FOR TEACHING AND LEARNING • DOI: 10.1002/tl

Implications for Future Research

There is a general lack of research on FGS on probation or who have been dismissed. The process of first-generation student identification being tied to financial aid does not provide faculty and university staff with adequate background information to assist these students. Faculty and advisers have no available way to identify FGS, and without such identification, they rely exclusively on FGS to disclose such information.

We encourage longitudinal studies of FGS on probation and dismissal. In the longitudinal survey, the same group of study participants would be studied over a specified length of time so that advisers could track the development of learning outcome competencies and institutional proficiency (McMillan, 2004). This study would allow the researchers to track students over the course of their collegiate careers and/or other endeavors. The study would not only highlight what students learn by being academically dismissed, but also track how they recover (or do not recover) from academic distress.

In conclusion, further data would allow researchers to discuss first-generation issues more specifically and understand better how to serve FGS in university environments.

References

Keeling, R. P. *Learning Reconsidered 2: A Practical Guide to Implementing a Campus-Wide Focus on the Student Experience.* Champaign, Ill.: Human Kinetics, 2006.
Kuh, G. *Student Learning Outside the Classroom: Transcending Artificial Boundaries.* Washington, D.C.: George Washington University, 1994.
McMillan, J. H. *Educational Research: Fundamentals for the Consumer.* (4th ed.). Boston: Pearson, 2004.

JENNIFER BROST *is an academic adviser in the College of Arts & Sciences at the University of Nebraska-Lincoln. She received her M.A. in educational administration with an emphasis in student affairs and a B.A. degree in communication studies from the University of Iowa. Her research interests include circumstances surrounding academic dismissal, learning outcomes in regard to student involvement on campus, and experiences of FGS.*

NEW DIRECTIONS FOR TEACHING AND LEARNING • DOI: 10.1002/tl

KELLY PAYNE *is a second-year Ph.D. student in the Department of English and academic adviser in the College of Arts & Sciences at the University of Nebraska-Lincoln. She received her M.A. in English literature from the University of Nebraska-Lincoln and her B.A. in English from Saint Mary's College in Indiana. Her primary research area is nineteenth-century American literature and reform, with a special interest in reform literature. In addition to her English scholarship, she examines academic affairs issues, specifically the causes and repercussions of academic dismissal and FGS' experiences. As a first-generation college graduate and academic, Payne strives to aid her first-generation advisees in the transition from high school to college. Her work has appeared in* National Academic Advising Association Journal *and* Encyclopedia of Contemporary LGBTQ Literature of the United States, *forthcoming from Greenwood Press. Currently, she is working on an article about Lydia Maria Child's short periodical fiction in the* Atlantic Monthly.

8

Drawing on interviews with first-generation college students (FGS), the author argues that the students' culture affects college attendance and success. Although FGS often have a vocational perspective to college, the author found that they seek meaningful work with good pay. The author also suggests that good decision making, academic preparation, and a strong social network (family, friends, teachers, and others) play a crucial role in helping FGS adjust to college.

A Social Constructionist View of Issues Confronting First-Generation College Students

Stephen Coffman

American culture tends to value the individual over the social. The country was founded on Enlightenment principles advocating autonomy for United States citizens and a minimum of governmental interference with private lives (Ellis and Esler, 1999). The Declaration of Independence and the Constitution were written to secure personal freedom and form a government to protect individuals' "natural" rights (Ellis and Esler). Consequently, in this competitive society Americans tend to accept democracy as a strategy for keeping citizens fairly and safely apart (Deetz, 1995).

In contrast to this dominant viewpoint, this chapter adopts a social constructionist framework to survey the first-generation college student–related literature. I advocate the perspective that culture influences college attendance and success. To detail these issues, I incorporate narratives from interviews with first-generation senior and graduate students attending a university in the Northwest.

According to Gadamer (1989), people interpret the meaning of cultural symbols through communication. Using Taylor and Van Every's (2000) model of an emergent communication process, I argue that there is a precipitating event, which is the conversation or talk in which people are engaged. Individuals derive personal meaning or an individual text from this talk. Narratives are repeated when some meanings or created realities are more attractive than others to some people.

NEW DIRECTIONS FOR TEACHING AND LEARNING, no. 127, Fall 2011 © Wiley Periodicals, Inc.
Published online in Wiley Online Library (wileyonlinelibrary.com) • DOI: 10.1002/tl.459

This chapter de-centers the individual and privileges the local culture, thus allowing an alternate standpoint acknowledging the impact of family, friends, teachers, counselors, and others on college experiences. The following discussion considers the complex human and social influences of race and class on first-generation college students' (FGS) college experiences.

Race and FGS

Walpole (2007) noted that race, gender, and class cannot be independently considered because FGS have numerous identities. Kim and Sax (2009) similarly found differences in the frequency of student–faculty interaction among students from different gender, race, social class, and first-generation status. Wartman and Savage (2008) also pointed to the effects of parent–student relationships in terms of gender, race, and socioeconomic class, with parents' educational level a heavy influence. In addition, Fischer (2007) reported that black and Hispanic students are more often FGS than their white or Asian counterparts, and they also tend to have lower socio-economic status backgrounds. Fischer added that the students also experience another disadvantage of being minorities on predominantly white campuses (see Kaba, 2008; Eitel and Martin, 2009; Tyler and Johns, 2009).

Some researchers suggest that media also influence college success. Bugeja (2004) argues that when people interpret reality through television and social networking sites, the world becomes flat because these media are two-dimensional. Judging others on these categories of race and class as represented in the media, and failing to use information from human interaction leads to inaccuracies and uncertainties. Consequently, Bugeja concludes that highly mediated persons tend to fear the unknown and react defensively, listen to protect self, and simplify reality (such as rich versus poor) when blaming others. The comments from the student interviews support these points:

"I believe that I grew up in a culture where there was a lack of hope. I grew up on the Blackfeet reservation, poverty stricken, cold, desolate area . . . "

"Through my family, friends, and people in high school, I found we often talk about college life; and of course, we have different atmosphere or topic to talk with people who do not go to college. I think a culture we live in has a huge impact on decision making."

"The media plays up college as being the only way you can make decent money when you grow up."

"College looked like one big party from a media standpoint. In movies and hearing about the football stars, it sounds like a perfect place! I will admit it is great, but nothing like the media portrays it to be."

"I think the media makes college look like one big party. They don't show the countless hours of blood, sweat and tears that go into obtaining a degree. That would be way too monotonous for TV or the news."

Lower Educational Aspirations

Researchers argue that family background heavily influences educational aspirations (Terenzini and Rendon, 1994). Primarily, Orbe (2004) notes that FGS often lack significant sense of communal identity. Terenzini, Pascarella, and Blimling (1996) found that FGS had lower educational aspirations than their second-generation counterparts. Terenzini's study (1996) also reported that FGS have lower family income and support. Moreover, Warburton, Bugarin, and Nunez (2001) observed that FGS are less likely to remain enrolled in a four-year institution or be on a track to a bachelor's degree. The students said in the interviews:

"College was not a big deal in my family, most of my relatives are not college graduates and going to college was not a concern for my parents, so it was impressed upon me pretty early on that it didn't matter to them what I did and that definitely limited my possibilities."

"My husband never finished his degree because he does not know what to do with his life."

"I come from a large family and by the time the last of us needed to get out of the house there was no talk about going to college or bettering our lives, just moving out."

"I am an only child and my mother was supportive from the beginning, but as years passed it hasn't been an issue whether I finished or not."

Poor Choices

Lack of critical thinking or decision-making skills usually accompany and negatively influence academic success. For example, Roth and others (2009) and Stoler (2007) argue that childhood problems can lead to poor decision making. Further, Langhout, Drake, and Rosselli (2009) noted that a person's developmental history correlates with dropout rates. Additionally, family background can influence the mistakes FGS make in choosing high school courses, managing time, and not knowing how to perform the student role (Collier, 2008). The respondents said:

"I have created a mess for myself. I am currently unemployed and hoping that having a bachelor's degree will open doors for me."

"However, the fact that I didn't finish what I started in 1988 has weighed heavily on me for many years."

"I think I rebelled against it. I was given every opportunity to finish college in the 1990s. I thought I knew best and now that I look back on so many decisions that I made, I wish I would have listened to my parents."

"Most of my friends did not go to college and are struggling financially. Generally, they make about half of what I make because they are not in skilled positions."

"By having completed my degree, it will give me the ability to open many doors for myself that could be closed otherwise."

"I decided I didn't want to hate my life and job for the rest of my life and that it was time to take advantage of the brain I was given and put it to work for me."

Social Class and FGS

Studies assert that low-income levels strongly influence factors such as having a support network, college debt, and degree completion. Smith (2008) found that students of lower socioeconomic status have reduced access to college and are increasingly marginalized on campuses. If FGS attend college, poorer students frequently leave with debt and no degree (Howard and Levine, 2004). Ishitani (2006) described a correlation between income levels and graduation probability. Also, lower-income students receiving grants rather than loans had higher graduation rates. In another study, Callender and Jackson (2008) observed a positive relationship between lower social class and college choice, in that poorer students tend to choose colleges located in less-expensive communities. Further, Lehmann (2009) noted that working-class youth tend to have utilitarian and vocational orientations toward college. Because of these factors that inhibit college success, other studies emphasize the importance of having a support network. For instance, Lindholm (2006) suggests that lack of support and even media can negatively affect FGS' view of college. Moschetti and Hudley (2008) argue that working-class FGS need to be encouraged to communicate with institutional professionals through e-mail and face-to-face interaction. The interviewees confirmed the previous studies' findings.

"I grew up in the working class culture and thought the only way to make a million dollars was to work a million hours."

"Well, the history in which my parents never attended college has informed and limited my possibilities. The way in which it limits them I suppose would be financially. They are not in a situation where they can help me pay for school . . . "

"My father was a ranch hand who moved from ranch to ranch until he passed away due to a ranching accident. My father had nothing to show for all his years of hard labor."

"If I were to have grown up in a family where everyone was a doctor or a lawyer instead of a rancher, welder, and teacher/councilor, I might be interested in a higher degree . . . "

"The limits to my possibilities would have been huge financially without the scholarships I received."

"My sister tried college but dropped out. She didn't influence my view. They (my family) think it's cool, but I think they are all waiting to see what I do with it. My friends think it is great also. They are supportive and wonder how I do it with two jobs and three kids."

Academic Preparation

Researchers suggest that FGS tend to be poorly prepared academically in high school (Terenzini, Pascarella, and Blimling, 1996). This factor often accompanies lower family incomes and lower high school engagement, which influence college success (Martinez, Sher, Krull, and Wood, 2009). Participation in a rigorous academic curriculum is essential for success (Choy, 2001; Warburton, Bugarin, and Nunez, 2001; Adelman, 2006). Anticipatory socialization also appears to precede college success (Attinasi, 1989). Using interviews with FGS, Reid (2007) found that most students said they did not develop the study skills in high school that would have helped them in college. In addition, Penrose (2002) observed that FGS differed from non-FGS in general academic preparedness, retention rates, and perceptions of their academic literacy skills. This study's respondents also affirm these notions.

"My younger sister tried college right after high school graduation and she wasn't ready so she put it off for now, it has been over fifteen years; maybe she will go back again someday."

"I consented to an environment that impressed upon me that I didn't need to have a college education, I just had to get by and did so until I made the decision that I deserved better and was going to take the time in my late twenties to complete my higher education."

"Teachers I had from high school gave the perception of not caring if their students went on to college."

"I realized that at the larger university I attended I was a nobody and I had come from a small school where I was at the top of the class and a successful student. I didn't like being average and unforgettable. I let too many professors get to me and tell me I'd never be as good as . . ."

Strong Social Network

Many studies emphasize the importance of a social network. Reid (2007) analyzed an education program designed to improve the academic performance of first-generation urban students. She found that students who succeeded "developed a strong social network, including both the family members and the school personnel that assisted them in accessing postsecondary education" (p. 104). Reid's study also suggested teachers were an important part of the students' social network. Fullilove and Treisman (1990) reported that requiring study groups in a calculus class improved black students' test scores. Other research asserts the positive relationship between parental involvement and educational aspirations (McCarron, Pagliarulo, and Kurotsuchi, 2006). Including parents in the educational process not only boosts students' aspirations, but also diminishes the negative effects of college culture shock. Martinez and Klopott (2005), Trusty and Niles (2004), and Wimberly and Noeth (2004) point to the importance of the family and school personnel in helping FGS prepare for college. Fann, Jarsky, and McDonough (2009) described a collaborative venture between a university education department and local schools that helped parents of FGS become active participants in their children's college preparation. Finally, Barry, Hudley, Kelly, and Cho (2009) cited a need for students to have opportunities to share stressful college-related experiences with others. The students' feedback reasserts these findings.

"I hate family functions because everyone discusses the successes of the college graduates and then when they talked about me, well I have great kids."

"Most of my friends are very academically driven. They are part of the reason I started school. As cliché as this sounds, going to college is the thing to do. I was able to be around my friends while working on school. I suppose they are my friends because our lives are similar. We attend school full-time, work full-time, have relationships, etc. In essence, we are fighting the same battle, we want to stick together. They can also be encouraging when school gets to me."

". . . the school was too large to for me to get personal with any of my instructors. My present school has been much different."

". . . others (like those who do not have or want a degree) don't understand that me finishing a paper is more important than watching a football game with them."

"My wife has been hugely supportive of me going back to school, she is one of the primary reasons I am focused today and have the desire to finish quickly."

"Also, my grandfather was a large influence on attending and succeeding in college. He is such a smart person, but dropped out of high school to marry my grandmother (she was pregnant, but we don't talk about that)."

"After struggling with substance abuse issues, my older brother got his life together and is now attending Gonzaga on a full-ride scholarship. He has inspired me to finish college. His story is incredible. At one time, he was actually homeless, abusing drugs, and nearly died as a result of this lifestyle. He is now working full time, raising a son by himself, and going to college."

Upward Social Mobility and Meaningful Work

Researchers argue that social class inspires students to have meaningful careers with better incomes. Lindholm's (2006) study supports the combined effects of societal, institutional, and relational dynamics in producing differential educational outcomes and post–high school life paths. Her findings indicated that culture, the particular institution, and relational support together influence FGS' college success. Richardson and Skinner (1992) and Terenzini, Pascarella, and Blimling (1996) found that FGS want to do better than their parents. FGS, like their non-first-generation peers, seek personally meaningful work (McKnight and Kashdan, 2009). The baccalaureate degree is a means toward upward social mobility, representing the single most important rung in the educational-attainment ladder in terms of economic benefits (Pascarella and Terenzini, 1991). However, Lehmann (2009) reported that poorer students often have a vocational notion of how college can increase economic status. The respondents similarly reported:

"My parents really wanted me to attend school because they thought it would be a great opportunity for me. They also wanted me to be able to do things they were not able to do, and have a better life with more opportunities."

"My reason for attending college is because I want to get a job that can support me and a family."

"My parents strived for me to have a better education than they. They did everything in their power financially and supportively to make my dream come true."

NEW DIRECTIONS FOR TEACHING AND LEARNING • DOI: 10.1002/tl

"Seeing my parents work at factories for most of my life showed me that I did not want to earn a living that way; having minimum wage jobs throughout high school and most of college also reinforced the need to advance my place in society."

Conclusion

Many of the 10 million jobs created over the next decade will require skills and competencies beyond those acquired in high school (Callan and Kratochwill, 2000). More FGS will go to college and graduate school, but it is difficult to predict individual first-generation student behavior and outcomes. As the literature and interviews indicate, FGS respond to race and class in complex ways. However, taken together, the studies and interviews affirm how programs servicing FGS must decrease marginalization because of race on campuses and also strengthen college preparation and support networks. Programs should also consider students' desire to exceed their parents' economic status and find meaningful work. By understanding the social influences on FGS' college experiences and success, family, advisers, college professionals, faculty, and others will be better positioned to successfully co-create strategies for college attendance and success.

References

Adelman, C. *The Toolbox Revisited: Paths to Degree Completion from High School Through College*. Washington, D.C.: U.S. Department of Education, 2006.

Attinasi, L. C. "Getting In: Mexican Americans' Perceptions of University Attendance and the Implications for Freshman Year Persistence." *Journal of Higher Education,* 1989, *60*(3), 247–277.

Barry, L. M. Hudley, C., Kelly, M., and Cho. S. J. "Differences in Self-Reported Disclosure of College Experiences by First-Generation College Student Status." *Adolescence,* 2009, *44*(173), 55.

Bugeja, M. *Interpersonal Divide: The Search for Community in a Technological Age*. New York: Oxford University Press, 2004.

Callan, K., and Kratochwill, T. R. "Empirically Supported Interventions and School Psychology: Rationale and Methodological Issues—Part I." *School Psychology Quarterly,* 2000, *15*(1), 75-105.

Callender, C., and Jackson, J. "Does the Fear of Debt Constrain Choice of University and Subject of Study?" *Studies in Higher Education,* 2008, *33*(4), 405–429.

Choy, S. *Students Whose Parents Did Not Go to College: Postsecondary Access, Persistence, and Attainment. Findings from the Condition of Education*, 2001. Retrieved November 8, 2009, from http://domex.nps.edu/corp/files/govdocs1.

Collier, P., and Morgan, D. "Is That Paper Really Due Today? Differences in First-Generation and Traditional College Students' Understandings of Faculty Expectations." *Higher Education,* 2008, *55*(4), 425–446.

Deetz, S. *Transforming Communication, Transforming Business: Building Responsive and Responsible Workplaces*. Cresskill, N.J.: Hampton Press, 1995.

Eitel, S. J., and Martin, J. "First-Generation Female College Students' Financial Literacy: Real and Perceived Barriers to Degree Completion." *College Student Journal,* 2009, *43*(2), 616.

Ellis, E., and Esler, A. *World History–Connections to Today–The Modern Era.* Englewood Cliffs, N.J.: Prentice Hall, 1999.

Fann, A., Jarsky, K. M., and McDonough, P. M. "Parent Involvement in the College Planning Process: A Case Study of p-20 Collaboration." *Journal of Hispanic Higher Education,* 2009, 8(4), 374–393.

Fischer, M. J. "Settling into Campus Life: Differences by Race/Ethnicity in College Involvement and Outcomes." *Journal of Higher Education,* 2007, 78(2), 125.

Fullilove, R. E., and Treisman, P. U. "Mathematics Achievement among African American Undergraduates at the University of California, Berkeley: An Evaluation of the Mathematics Workshop." *The Journal of Negro Education,* 1990, 59(3), 463–478.

Gadamer, H. G. *Truth and Method.* New York: Crossroad, 1989.

Howard, A., and Levine, A. "Where Are the Poor Students? A Conversation about Social Class and College Attendance." *About Campus,* 2004, 9(4),19–24.

Ishitani, T. T. "Studying Attrition and Degree Completion Behavior among First-Generation College Students in the United States." *Journal of Higher Education,* 2006, 77(5), 861.

Kaba, A. J. "Race, Gender and Progress: Are Black American Women the New Model Minority?" *Journal of African American Studies,* 2008, 12(4), 309.

Kim, Y., and Sax, L. "Student–Faculty Interaction in Research Universities: Differences by Student Gender, Race, Social Class, and First-Generation Status." *Research in Higher Education,* 2009, 50(5), 437–459.

Langhout, R. D., Drake, P., and Rosselli, F. "Classism in the University Setting: Examining Student Antecedents and Outcomes." *Journal of Diversity in Higher Education,* 2009, 2(3), 166–181.

Lehmann, W. "University as Vocational Education: Working-Class Students' Expectations for University." *British Journal of Sociology of Education,* 2009, 30(2), 137–149.

Lindholm, J. A. "Deciding to Forgo College: Non-College Attendees' Reflections on Family, School, and Self." *Teachers College Record,* 2006, 108(4), 577–603.

Martinez, J. A., Sher, K. J., Krull, J. L., and Wood, P. K. "Blue-Collar Scholars?: Mediators and Moderators of University Attrition in First-Generation College Students." *Journal of College Student Development,* 2009, 50(1), 87–103.

Martinez, M., and Klopott, S. *The Link between High School Reform and College Access and Success for Low-Income and Minority Youth.* Washington, D.C.: American Youth Policy Forum and Boston, Mass: Pathways to College Network, Education Resources Institute, 2005. Retrieved November 8, 2009, from https://dst.sp.maricopa.edu/DWG/STPG/ JuniorACE/ Shared %20 HS%20reform%20and %20college%20access%20 and%20success%20for%20lo.pdf.

McCarron, G., Pagliarulo, I., and Kurotsuchi, K. "The Gap between Educational Aspirations and Attainment for First-Generation College Students and the Role of Parental Involvement." *Journal of College Student Development,* 2006, 47(5), 534–549.

McKnight, P. E., and Kashdan, T. B. "Purpose in Life as a System that Creates and Sustains Health and Well-Being: An Integrative, Testable Theory." *Review of General Psychology: Journal of Division 1, of the American Psychological Association,* 2009, 13(3), 242.

Moschetti, R., and Hudley, C. "Measuring Social Capital among First-Generation and Non-First-Generation, Working-Class, White Males." *Journal of College Admission,* 2008, 4(198), 25–30.

Orbe, M. P. "Negotiating Multiple Identities within Multiple Frames: An Analysis of First-Generation College Students." *Communication Education,* 2004, 53(2), 131.

Pascarella, E.T., and Terenzini, P. T. *How College Affects Students: Findings and Insights from Twenty Years of Research.* San Francisco: Jossey-Bass, 1991.

Penrose, A. M. "Academic Literacy Perceptions and Performance: Comparing First-Generation and Continuing-Generation College Students." *Research in the Teaching of English,* 2002, *36*(4), 437–461.

Reid, M. J. "First-Generation Urban College Students Speaking Out about Their Secondary School Preparation for Postsecondary Education." Unpublished doctoral dissertation, 2007. The Ohio State University. Retrieved January 16, 2010, from http://etd.ohiolink.edu/send- pdf.cgi/Reid%20M.%20 Jeanne.pdf.

Richardson, R. J., and Skinner, E. F. "Helping First-Generation Minority Students Achieve Degrees." *New Directions for Community Colleges,* 1992, *80*(4), 29–43.

Roth, G., and others. "The Emotional and Academic Consequences of Parental Conditional Regard: Comparing Conditional Positive Regard, Conditional Negative Regard, and Autonomy Support as Parenting Practices." *Developmental Psychology,* 2009, *45*(4), 1119–1142.

Smith, M. J. "College Choice Process of First Generation Black Female Students: Encouraged to What End?" *Negro Educational Review,* 2008, *59*(3–4), 147.

Stoler, B. (2007). "A 'Mistake' Leads To Business School; Having Learned a Lot from One Wrong Turn, I Applied to Only One B-School—But It Was the Perfect One for Me." *Business Week Online,* Oct. 9, 2007.

Taylor, J. R., and Van Every, E. J. *The Emergent Organization: Communication as Its Site and Surface.* Mahwah, N.J.: Erlbaum, 2000.

Terenzini, P. T., Pascarella, E. T., and Blimling, G. S. "Students' Out-of-Class Experiences and Their Influence on Learning and Cognitive Development: A Literature Review." *Journal of College Student Development,* 1996, *37*(2), 149–162.

Terenzini, P. T., and Rendon, L. I. The Transition to College: Diverse Students, Diverse Stories. *Research in Higher Education,* 1994, *35*(1), 57–74.

Trusty, J., and Niles, S. G. "Realized Potential or Lost Talent: High School Variables and Bachelor's Degree Completion." *Career Development Quarterly,* 2004, *53*(1), 2–16.

Tyler, M. D., and Johns, K. Y. "From First-Generation College Student to First Lady." *Diverse: Issues in Higher Education,* 2009, *25*(25), 19.

Walpole, M. E. "Economically and Educationally Challenged Students in Higher Education: Access to Outcomes." *ASHE Higher Education Report,* 2007, *33*(3), 1–113.

Warburton, E. C., Bugarin, R., and Nunez, A. "Bridging the Gap: Academic Preparation and Postsecondary Success of First Generation College Students." Washington, DC: National Center for Educational Statistics, 2001.

Wartman, K. L., and Savage, M. "Parental Involvement in Higher Education: Understanding the Relationship among Students, Parents, and the Institution." *ASHE Higher Education Report,* 2008, *33*(6), 1–125.

Wimberly, J. L., and Noeth, R. J. *Schools Involving Parents in Early Postsecondary Planning. ACT Policy Report.* Iowa City, Iowa: ACT, 2004.

STEPHEN COFFMAN *is a professor of communication at Montana State University-Billings. He has served as chair of his department for twelve years. He holds a Ph.D. and M.A. in communication studies from the University of Kansas. He earned a bachelor's degree in psychology from the University of Rochester. His research areas include language use and power issues in organizational communication and communication and aging. He has published in such journals as the* Journal of Applied Communication Research, Omega: Journal of Death and Dying, Small Group Behavior, *and the* Association for Communication Administration Bulletin. *He has also consulted for over 100 nonprofit professional organizations.*

*Informed by Rosenberg's (2003) concept of nonviolent communica-
tion, the author's pedagogical perspective encourages educators to
criticize institutional and classroom practices that ideologically
place underserved students at disadvantaged positions. At the same
time, this perspective urges teachers to be self-reflective of their
actions through compassion as a daily commitment. The author suggests that this pedagogical approach helps teachers better counter
institutional barriers and oppressive pedagogical practices that
inhibit first-generation college students' success.*

Critical Compassionate Pedagogy and the Teacher's Role in First-Generation Student Success

Richie Neil Hao

A week before fall semester of 2005 started, I attended my departmental
orientation and discovered that the department offers sections of oral communication for The Center for Academic Success (CAS) students. In one
orientation session, the director of the CAS program mentioned that CAS
students, who are mainly first-generation college students (FGS) of color,
do not get admitted into the Midwestern public university because of low
SAT or ACT scores, but they are specially admitted to the CAS program
because of their potential to succeed; that is, despite low standardized test
scores, these students have good grade point averages (GPAs) and participated in school activities. Of the approximately 150 FGS at the university,
many are enrolled in the CAS program (*Minority, Women and Disabled*,
2008). Therefore, in this chapter, when I speak of "first-generation students," I focus on CAS students who are FGS and are primarily students of
color from Chicago, East St. Louis, and rural southern Illinois. In addition,
the director informed us that many FGS are not academically prepared
compared to other matriculated students.

After the orientation session ended, I started working on my syllabi for
two different sections of oral communication—one for FGS and another for
non-FGS. Even though both classes had the same course requirements and
class schedule, I made a mental note that FGS have different pedagogical

NEW DIRECTIONS FOR TEACHING AND LEARNING, no. 127, Fall 2011 © Wiley Periodicals, Inc.
Published online in Wiley Online Library (wileyonlinelibrary.com) • DOI: 10.1002/tl.460

needs compared to their peers, which prompted me to rethink my pedagogy. Influenced by Fassett and Warren's (2007) work on critical communication pedagogy, my commitment to FGS was engaging myself in what I call "critical compassionate pedagogy," which is a pedagogical commitment that allows educators to criticize institutional and classroom practices that ideologically place underserved students at disadvantaged positions, while at the same time be self-reflexive of their actions through compassion as a daily commitment.

Drawing from Rosenberg's (2003) nonviolent communication (also known as compassionate communication), which aims for people to listen compassionately and express themselves in ways that are likely to receive a compassionate response in others, I attempt to use critical compassionate pedagogy as a pedagogical framework by intersecting compassionate communication with critical pedagogy. Critical pedagogy deals "not only with questions of schooling, curriculum, and educational policy but also with social justice and human possibility" (Kincheloe, 2005, p. 7). Although critical pedagogy critiques oppressive educational practices, it does not explicitly communicate that it is essential for educators to be compassionate. Therefore, this chapter's purpose is to reflect on my experiences teaching FGS, and implement a pedagogy that stresses the importance for educators to be both critical and compassionate in the classroom. Implementing critical compassionate pedagogy is important because, realistically and practically speaking, many teachers do not consider the pedagogical needs of underserved student populations that often could negatively affect the students' likelihood to succeed in the academy. So, as critical compassionate pedagogues, we should be critical of institutional barriers and current oppressive pedagogical practices, and be compassionate as teachers to help FGS succeed.

Compassionate Communication

Rosenberg's (2003) compassionate communication is "founded on language and communication skills that strengthen our ability to remain human, even under trying conditions . . . [it] trains us to observe carefully, and to be able to specify behaviors and conditions that are affecting us" (p. 3). In addition, compassionate communication emphasizes the importance of minimizing resistance, defensiveness, and violent reactions. Rosenberg also highlights that compassionate communication does not always happen quickly, but rather is a process.

Compassionate communication involves the following four components: observation, feeling, need, and request. Observation is the intent to observe without making an initial judgment or evaluation. During the observation process, "we observe what is actually happening in a situation: what are we observing others are saying or doing that is either enriching or not enriching our life" (Rosenberg, 2003, p. 6). In other words, observation allows participants to establish common ground by not judging or evaluating and remaining open to clarify behaviors and conditions that are affecting us.

Second, compassionate communication is about expressing one's feelings and asking ourselves if we are hurt, scared, joyful, amused, irritated, etc. According to Rosenberg (2003), expressing feelings tends to increase connection between people. Unlike thinking, expressing our feelings enables us to identify and communicate in ways that do not imply judgment, criticism, or blame toward others.

Third, compassionate communication connects our needs to the feelings we have identified. We should also ask ourselves what needs, values, and desires create the feelings we have. Rosenberg (2003) points out that needs are universal, shared, and the root of our feelings. By identifying our needs to each other, we create an understanding that allows us to move toward the process of becoming.

The last component of compassionate communication concerns a specific request; its purpose is to clarify what has been heard and/or seen; what people are feeling; and what action should be used to meet the needs without trying to motivate the other party out of guilt, fear, or obligation (Rosenberg, 2003). More important, because requests do not have conditions, participants have an opportunity to evaluate and decide whether or not to fulfill such needs.

Critical Compassionate Pedagogy and FGS

After providing an overview of compassionate communication, I will intersect its four components with critical pedagogy to understand how educators and FGS can improve their pedagogical interactions. Although critical compassionate pedagogy is not the only pedagogical framework that can be used to help FGS succeed academically, I will use it as a pedagogical possibility to discuss what we can do as educators to enhance FGS' academic experience.

Observation

As Rosenberg (2003) states, observation is the intent to observe without making an initial judgment or evaluation. As I recall my encounter with the CAS program, I learned that FGS have been (stereo)typically categorized as at-risk students, who are perceived as students that need to be fixed, intervened, and saved (Fassett and Warren, 2005). Part of their perceived at-riskness has to do with many FGS coming from lower socioeconomic and racial minority backgrounds. Due to systemic and institutional barriers in education, the director also pointed out that many FGS do not have foundational reading and writing skills, which could prevent them from enrolling in classes with other students.

After hearing about FGS, I learned that many need teachers who are willing to help them succeed. Keeping the first component of compassionate communication in mind, critical educators must observe FGS' learning styles in the classroom and how they interact with teachers and peers. For instance, on the first day of class, I typically ask students to introduce themselves and talk about their likes and dislikes about different approaches to pedagogy. Some of the questions I ask on the first day are: Are you a visual learner? Would it help for me to write important concepts on the board? Is conducting the class in a seminar format (i.e., discussion based) more conducive to your learning style than a lecture format? Why or why not? Does it help to show visual media to supplement class readings? I also ask students to fill out a questionnaire to find out what pedagogical accommodations they need. For example, I ask if their work and transportation schedules could sometimes result in coming to class a few minutes late. Because many FGS, especially FGS of color, have part-time jobs and rely on other means to get to school, I need to consider certain pedagogical accommodations to help alleviate some challenges these students face while juggling school and other responsibilities. By doing so, my students and I will have an open communication that allows me to help them succeed academically. My first-generation college students, in particular, appreciate me asking these questions to observe their pedagogical needs; in fact, such class discussion allows us to frankly talk about what I can do as a teacher to help them learn.

Feeling

After observing what kinds of student populations we have in our classrooms, we must identify our feelings toward students' needs. Asking about our feelings is not simply about probing if we are happy or sad; the purpose is to ask why we feel FGS continue to be underserved in higher education. For instance, as educators, we need to first be honest and ask ourselves how we feel about teaching FGS. Do we feel it is going to be challenging to have FGS in our classroom? Do we think it is not necessary to make pedagogical adjustments to cater to FGS? It is perfectly all right to be unsure, but we must ask ourselves why we feel the way we do. Critical compassionate pedagogy is about asking the tough questions—questions that we sometimes do not want to confront.

By asking our feelings toward FGS' needs, we can investigate our perceptions of FGS. When I first heard of FGS, I had false assumptions that all are from the inner-city, have poor grades, and/or are not prepared for college. I met FGS who were white, came from middle-class families, lived in rural areas, and were "A" students. After learning that FGS come from diverse backgrounds, I realized how important it is to ask why we feel it may be a challenge to teach FGS; such questions can allow us—as it allowed me—to also examine who we are as pedagogues and our own "positionalities" and privileges in the academy and society.

NEW DIRECTIONS FOR TEACHING AND LEARNING • DOI: 10.1002/tl

I think it is important that we should care about examining our feelings toward FGS because we must be prepared to teach them in our classrooms. If all we perceive of FGS is that they are at-risk and are likely to fail, then we are not prepared to teach them. In that case, it might be more beneficial for students to have a teacher who truly cares about and understands them. Before I decided to teach a section of oral communication that was designed primarily for FGS, I had to seriously ask myself if I could handle teaching this special section as a novice teacher. As I was told at the orientation meeting, I had to devote extra time to accommodate the needs of FGS, especially helping them with writing skills because many came from high schools without the resources to prepare them for college. So, asking to see if I was prepared enough to teach FGS is important to better serve these students. Because I was honest enough to confront my feelings toward teaching FGS, I have succeeded in overcoming some of the initial negative stereotypes I may have had about them by being able to acknowledge that they are not stupid or lazy (as they have often been stereotyped), but rather that many did not have the same opportunities as their peers.

With that said, critical compassionate pedagogues must engage their feelings toward the lack of academic support of FGS with what they can do pedagogically to enhance the students' academic experience. Although the process of asking how we feel about our current approach to pedagogy seems like asking a lot, the process is really about self-reflection and acknowledgment that there is something we can do to help and support FGS.

Need

With our knowledge of how we feel about meeting the needs of FGS, we must ask what we need from our students and vice versa to create a culturally inclusive pedagogy. To understand our needs as well as our students', we need to ask some important questions: What kinds of pedagogy do we need to develop to help FGS succeed? What do our FGS need from us to succeed in our classroom? Before I started teaching FGS, I thought about the same questions I mentioned above to involve myself and my students in a pedagogy that values their presence. In that process, I discovered and acknowledged that my FGS were different from students in other classes based on their cultural, ethnic, racial, linguistic, socioeconomic, and educational backgrounds. With that knowledge in mind, I needed to develop different pedagogical practices, such as including FGS' experiences in my class assignments. For example, in the cultural narrative speech assignment, I required my students to talk about what culture means in communicating their identity; "culture" could be broadly defined as race, gender, class, educational background, etc. So, I told my students that if they were FGS, I encouraged them to talk about their experience and the perceptions that come along with being a first-generation student. The cultural narrative assignment allowed me to incorporate the voices of my FGS in the curriculum that often get silenced or ignored. More important, it empowered my FGS to continue to believe that they belong in the academy.

Even though marking FGS as "different" may sound like naming them as academically challenged, especially in the public presentation of their educational background, acknowledging their "difference" is actually a confrontation that different structural and cultural barriers exist that could affect FGS academically, such as the fact that inequalities in education exist that could privilege certain educational bodies while oppress others like FGS. In addition, as teachers, we also need to indicate what we need from our FGS to help them achieve their academic goals. For instance, right before speech presentation days, I made an effort to talk to my FGS about practicing their speeches with me to make sure that they are at least meeting the minimum requirements of the assignments. Additionally, if I noticed that they seem to have trouble with class for some reason, I would have a talk with my FGS about potential issues. By providing different academic services to my FGS, I made a conscious choice to acknowledge that they have pedagogical needs that warrant attention.

Request

Perhaps most important, critical compassionate pedagogues need to clarify what they have observed, felt, and needed by engaging in pedagogical actions to meet the needs of FGS. For FGS to succeed academically, critical compassionate pedagogues need to develop an open communication with their students. We often forget how critical it is for educators to ask students what we can do to better serve their needs and enhance their academic experience. I cannot stress enough the importance of reminding ourselves that we can always do something pedagogically to help our FGS.

Unfortunately, many FGS are too afraid to ask for help because they think that teachers may perceive them as unprepared for college. In that regard, we need to emphasize that we are here to help, but we cannot help them without them providing us feedback. I made a conscious effort to talk to my FGS individually during office hours to discuss their progress in class and ask them if I have met their pedagogical needs. For instance, I would inquire about whether or not my approach to pedagogy works for my FGS. Some of the questions I asked were: Is the pace of the class working for them? How are the readings so far? Do they face significant challenges with the assignments? Although these questions can also be applied to non-FGS, I found that it was particularly helpful to motivate FGS because they often face a lot of pressure to succeed in college. The pressure could build up in having a terrible college experience, so my commitment in providing FGS extra academic support is another way for me to let them know that I want them to succeed, but to achieve that they must let me know how I can assist them.

NEW DIRECTIONS FOR TEACHING AND LEARNING • DOI: 10.1002/tl

Furthermore, some of my FGS experienced tragic or difficult circumstances while attending school, such as losing a family member and facing an unstable financial situation. Although non-FGS could also experience similar situations, I argue that FGS are more vulnerable than their other peers. For instance, they may not have a lot of family members who understand or support their academic endeavors that could result in encouraging them to drop out to support their family financially. Some of these students' families expressed that they are wasting their time in school instead of working to help their family's financial situation. Whenever necessary to respond to unexpected circumstances, I make every effort to meet with students to discuss possible options that could help them remain in class. Making special accommodations for my students is one possible option, such as giving them extra time to complete their assignments.

There is no doubt that allowing open communication between me and my students is a significant contribution to my own pedagogical development. Rosenberg (2003) states that the other party does not necessarily need to communicate compassionately for compassionate communication to work. Regardless, we must ask our students what they can do to become the best they can be not only for the course, but also for their overall personal, academic, and professional development. As much as we want to accommodate the pedagogical needs of our FGS, we must always motivate them to do better. After all, completing the course is one thing; succeeding in the academy is another.

Because there are so many unwritten rules of the academy that FGS must learn on their own without the parental or family guidance that their peers typically have, we must serve as mentors to these students. In so many ways, reflecting from Freire's work on critical pedagogy (2000), critical compassionate pedagogy is also about allowing our students to become subjects (rather than objects) in the pedagogical process. In sum, critical compassionate pedagogy is not a pedagogical destination, but rather a process where both students and teachers are engaged in creating pedagogy where cultural difference is valued in the classroom.

Conclusion

I introduced critical compassionate pedagogy to make us realize that we need to be critical of the inequality of our classrooms and move toward a pedagogy that allows open communication between students and teachers. Critical compassionate pedagogy is also about examining our feelings toward FGS' pedagogical needs, which enables us to be critical of cultural, racial, linguistic, and socioeconomic disparities that exist in education.

Furthermore, critical compassionate pedagogy is about involving both educators and students in talking about their needs to establish a pedagogy that works for both of them. Teachers can try to implement different approaches to pedagogy to cater to the needs of a diverse student body.

Teachers can also provide extra academic support to FGS, which can be a great help to those who are struggling with course materials, but are too afraid to ask for help. Unfortunately, many FGS end up failing because they are too embarrassed to ask questions for fear of being perceived as unprepared. Although teachers must ensure that they are meeting the needs of FGS, students themselves should also strive to become the best students they can be.

I remember the day when I first stepped into my CAS classroom. I realized then to treat my FGS with more compassion while also becoming critical of how I approach my pedagogy. For example, I became more compassionate when students could not turn in class assignments due to unforeseen circumstances. Instead of not accepting late work, I made necessary arrangements with students to complete assignments. I also included more visual and aural components to my pedagogy, which would allow students with different learning abilities to do well in my class. Although these approaches may not work for everyone, I believe that we must be willing to help our students in any way we can.

My hope for writing about critical compassionate pedagogy is to make us rethink our own pedagogy. We often fail to realize that our education system has failed many students from the start, and we need to make an effort in giving our compassion as teachers to help them succeed academically. It is important to note, however, that critical compassionate pedagogy is not a "feel good pedagogy"; it is about our critical engagement in the education process of FGS (and other marginalized students) by committing to better serve their needs that can hopefully allow them to someday say, "I am the first one to make it."

References

Fassett, D. L., and Warren, J. T. "The Strategic Rhetoric of an "At-Risk" Educational Identity: Interviewing Jane." *Communication and Critical/Cultural Studies*, 2005, 2, 238–256.

Fassett, D. L., and Warren, J. T. *Critical Communication Pedagogy*. Thousand Oaks, Calif.: Sage, 2007.

Freire, P. *Pedagogy of the Oppressed: 30th Anniversary Edition.* New York: Continuum, 2000. (Original work published in 1970.)

Kincheloe, J. L. *Critical Pedagogy Primer.* New York: Peter Lang, 2005.

Minority, Women and Disabled Students, Faculty and Staff: Annual Report. Carbondale, Ill.: Southern Illinois University, Office of Academic Affairs, 2008.

Rosenberg, M. B. *Nonviolent Communication: A Language of Life.* (2nd ed.). Encinitas, Calif.: PuddleDancer Press, 2003.

RICHIE NEIL HAO *is an assistant professor in the Department of Communication Studies at the University of Denver. His research interests are at the intersections of intercultural, pedagogical, and performance studies. He previously served as the assistant director of the core curriculum in the Department of Speech Communication at Southern Illinois University, Carbondale.*

10

*Academic personnel who were first-generation college stu-
dents (FGS) are uniquely positioned to consider the questions
these students often have about the college experience.
Academia needs first-generation and working-class voices to
diversify an academic culture that is often socially stratified.
As more FGS enroll in colleges and universities, academic personnel must be prepared to better understand, and teach, this
growing demographic sector of undergraduate and graduate
students.*

Gathering Ourselves and Our Students: Concluding Remarks

Vickie L. Harvey, Teresa Heinz Housel

I (Vickie Harvey) came to college as a nontraditional first-generation college student. Growing up in Anchorage, Alaska, where my father was a
carpenter and my mother was an accountant at a bank, the supervisor actually, somehow I decided to go back to college in my late twenties. I worked
right out of high school as my parents did and figured working at a grocery
store, bank, or as a secretary was good enough for my parents and would be
good for me. They were both extremely successful in their jobs, and I
would succeed in a job as well.

At some point between my many jobs, my best friend invited me to the
University of Colorado, Boulder where she attended college. I went to class
with her once, and I was hooked. Hooked on learning, socializing, and
spending time with books rather than handling money at the grocery store
(my current gig). I enrolled the next semester and thus began my journey
as a first-generation college student.

My desire to learn and have the world open up in ways I'd never
dreamed of became my designation. I had always been an average student
in high school, preferring to socialize with my friends rather than sit in
boring classes listening to regurgitated lectures. I visited my high school
counselor as a first semester senior and told her I was thinking of dropping
out. She informed me that I had more than enough units to graduate early.
Off I went to join the workforce. After almost ten years in the workforce,
Paula, my best friend, opened a new door for me. It was one that I would
stay in for more than nine years earning my bachelor's, master's, and doctorate degrees.

NEW DIRECTIONS FOR TEACHING AND LEARNING, no. 127, Fall 2011 © Wiley Periodicals, Inc.
Published online in Wiley Online Library (wileyonlinelibrary.com) • DOI: 10.1002/tl.461

I always remember where I came from and how I started my educational journey. What surprises me is not that I am now a full professor at a university, but that my parents remained in their working class roles throughout their lives, although they retired years ago and my mother passed away in March 2010. I still remember my mother trying to understand the differences between assistant, associate, and full professor. If I am promoted to full, does that mean I can't be promoted again, and why is that? Why was my salary so low for having completed so *many* years of education? I remember her asking why I had to focus on research to be a teacher. Why do I spend so much time writing instead of teaching or interacting with students? Those are good questions for us to address, but that is a different book.

Teresa and I hope that the chapters in this edited book provided some answers to questions about first-generation college students (FGS) to those of us who teach, interact, and assist FGS. These are common questions we have encountered: How do FGS decide that college is their path to take? Although our parents are working class, or managers of their own business, or people who have figured out the employment system, how did we learn from our family of origin that college was an option for us? If we did not receive this message from our family, where did our messages to pursue higher education come from, and why did they have such a profound influence on us? Once introduced to college, how did we navigate our way into and through college to earn bachelor's degrees, and in many cases graduate degrees?

Many of us made it through college with the help of friends, family members, and university programs tailored to FGS. All of us made it through college by learning how to succeed in the educational system. The educational system is different from the working world, but there are similarities. You are evaluated by either supervisors or teachers (more teachers in college than supervisors unless you switched jobs frequently, which I did when the job become too boring and routine). You improve by listening and adapting to your boss or teacher. You change classes when the teacher or course content is not to your liking, much like how you change jobs. You learn to socialize with your peers, and through social networking you are rewarded with support to succeed in the environment of school or work.

I (Teresa Housel) long ago made peace with my working-class origins. I used to be ashamed of my background and tried to pass as fully middle-class. Gradually, I realized the ability to code-shift between social classes is a rare gift. I celebrate this gift with humility. This gift has allowed me to have success as a teacher and mentor because I am able to compassionately and effectively communicate with students from diverse backgrounds.

Because I still move between class circles, the life stories I learn from others serve as poignant and sometimes hilarious anecdotal examples in my classes. One Hope College student recently told me that I was different somehow from some of his other teachers because I shared real stories to illustrate complex theoretical concepts. Academia, which remains stratified by privileges of class, gender, and race, needs first-generation and working-class voices.

Our contributing authors shared their voices and research to their understanding of what it takes to succeed as FGS. We hope that readers will use this book's ideas to better understand and teach this underserved, but growing demographic of undergraduate and graduate students.

VICKIE L. HARVEY is a full professor in the Communication Studies Department at the California State University, Stanislaus. She conducts research and teaches courses that emphasize the importance of communicating in relationships. Her primary line of research focuses on cross-sex friendships and how platonic friends meet O'Meara's four challenges of remaining just friends. She and Dr. Heinz Housel published their first book, The Invisibility Factor: Administrators and Faculty Reach Out to First-Generation College Students *(BrownWalker Press), on first-generation college students and how administrative programs help FGS succeed in college. Her research has been published in* Sex Roles, Communication Teacher, Iowa Journal of Communication, The Qualitative Report, International Journal of Information and Communication Technology Education, The Academic Exchange Quarterly, *and* Readings in Gender Communication. *She is currently an editor for* The Academic Exchange Quarterly.

TERESA HEINZ HOUSEL is an associate professor of communication at Hope College in Holland, Michigan. While a first-generation college student at Oberlin College in the early 1990s, she became interested in how the academic environment culturally marginalizes many FGS. Her research in the areas of homelessness; the politics of housing; media and globalization; and language, power, and class have appeared in Critical Studies in Media Communication, Information, Communication & Society, *and* Journal of Critical Inquiry.

NEW DIRECTIONS FOR TEACHING AND LEARNING • DOI: 10.1002/tl

INDEX

Academic dismissal: applications of findings on, for faculty and staff, 77; and cognitive complexity, 71–73; findings from study on, 76–77; implications of study on, for future research, 78; interpersonal and intrapersonal questions regarding, 73–74; learning outcomes from testimonials on, 69–78; and practical competence, 74–76; study method for, 71
Academic preparation, 85–86
ACT, 85, 91; preparation classes, 34
Adelman, C., 85
African American students, 36, 82
Akande, Y., 8, 41
Allensworth, E., 34
Altman, I., 56
Ambler, M., 47
American Indian College Fund, 42
American Indian Higher Education Consortium, 41–43, 45–49; Conference, 48
Ancis, J., 57
Anticipating needs, gender-based role of, 27
Appalachian students, 45
Arellano, A., 24
Arenhall, D., 55
Arizona, 43
Armesto, M., 33
Ashburn, E., 43
Asian students, 82
Attinasi, L. C., 85

Barber, C., 46
Barefoot, B., 55
Barry, L. M., 86
Baxter, L., 56
Belonging, issues of, 25
Bermeo, A., 55
Blimling, G. S., 83, 85, 87
Bliss, J. R., 36
Bochner, A. P., 57
Borderland, motif of, 24
Braithwaite, C. A., 49
Braun, J., 42
Brooks-Terry, M., 55
Brost, J., 8–9, 69
Bugarin, R., 83, 85

Bugeja, M., 82
Bui, K. V., 7
Bureau of Indian Affairs, 45

California, 23
California State University, Stanislaus, 2
Callan, K., 88
Callender, C., 84
"Call-Response as Cultural Performance: Verbal Interaction among African American Movie Audience Members" (Graham), 36
Canary, D., 56
Cankdeska Cikana Community College, 47
CAS. See Center for Academic Success (CAS)
Cawyer, C. S., 36
Ceballo, R., 24
Center for Academic Success (CAS), 91
Challenger space shuttle explosion, 36
Chicana, 23
Cho, S. J., 86
Choy, S., 85
Cissna, K. N., 57
Code of Ethics (National Association of Social Workers), 28
Coffman, S., 9, 81
Cognitive complexity, 71–73
Coles, A. S., 33
Collier, P., 14, 51, 83
Communication, compassionate, 92–93
Correa, M., 34
Cox, D. E., 57
Crissman Ishler, J. L., 55
Culture, student: and academic preparation, 85–86; and lower educational aspirations, 83; and poor choices, 83–84; and race, 82–83; and social class, 84–85; and social constructivist view of first-generation college student issues, 81–88; and strong social network, 86–87; and upward mobility and meaningful work, 87–88
Cushman, K., 43, 47

Davis, D. M., 36
Declaration of Independence, 81

103

For a complete list of back issues, please visit www.josseybass.com/go/ndtl

Héfer Bembenutty
This volume reports new findings associating students' self-regulation
of learning with their academic achievement, motivation for learning,
and use of cognitive and learning strategies. Self-regulation of learning
is a hallmark of students' ability to remain goal-oriented while pursuing
academic-specific intentions in postsecondary education. Protecting such
long-term and temporally distant goals requires that college and university
students be proactive in directing their learning experiences, guide their own
behavior, seek help from appropriate sources, sustain motivation, and delay
gratification. The authors suggest how college students can control their
cognition and behavior to attain academic goals, select appropriate learning
strategies, and monitor and evaluate their academic progress.
This volume calls the attention of students and educators to the vital role
that self-regulation plays in every aspect of postsecondary education. The
contributors provide compelling evidence supporting the notion that
self-regulation is related to positive academic outcomes, such as delay of
gratification, self-efficacy beliefs, and use of cognitive strategies, and that it is
important for the training of teachers and school psychologists. The authors
offer diverse vantage points from which students, teachers, administrators,
and policy makers can orchestrate their efforts to empower students with
self-regulatory learning strategies, appropriate motivational beliefs, and
academic knowledge and skills.
ISBN: 978-11180-91630

Mathew L. Ouellett
College and university instructors continue to seek models that help
students to better understand today's complex social relationships. Feminist,
Queer, and Ethnic Studies scholars put forward compelling arguments for
more integrative understandings of race, class, gender, and sexuality and for
centering the experiences of women, people of color, and others traditionally
relegated to the margins. Intersectionality is one such approach.
In nine chapters, the contributors to this volume offer an overview of
key tenets of intersectionality and explore applications of this model in
faculty and instructional development in higher education. Gathered from
across the disciplines, they draw upon a range of approaches to social
identity formation, different theoretical models, and a complement of lived
experiences. When read together, these chapters offer a systemic approach to
change in higher education by addressing innovations at course, department,
and institutional levels.
Intersectionality does not advocate for a flattening of differences. Instead, it
argues for another layer of critical analyses that acknowledge the powerful
interplay of the many aspects of social identity to address the rapidly shifting
ways in which we talk about and describe identities in society and the
complexity of classroom dynamics in the academy today. By illuminating
the interconnected nature of systems of oppression, we shine a light on the
potential for disrupting the status quo and create stronger alliances for social
justice.
ISBN: 978-11180-27622

TL124   Experiential Education: Making the Most of Learning Outside
the Classroom
Donna M. Qualters
As the cost of education increases, endowments decline, and the job market
tightens, institutions of higher learning are faced with many challenges:
How do we remain relevant in a world where many still view us as the "ivory
tower"? If we bring in the outside world, how do we convince our own
faculty of its value in the classroom? How do we help students combine that
exposure with the deep reflection that will give them the knowledge and
skills necessary for their future?
Some of our most powerful learning experiences occur outside the
classroom. How should higher education institutions—and their
administrators, faculty, and staff—recognize, structure, encourage, and
supplement this direct engagement with productive work? This volume
addresses this question in the voices of veteran, passionate educators who
fervently believe in the value of learning from experience. Every day, each
of these authors incorporates extramural learning into their practice; in this
volume, they have contributed their insights into the forms of, issues within,
and operationalization of experiential education.
Experiential Education: Making the Most of Learning Outside the Classroom is
intended to aid administrators, faculty, and staff in the design, construction,
assessment, and funding of experiential education. From descriptions of
individual courses to the layout of entire programs, these writers address the
realities of experiential learning—the need to reflect upon its lessons and
engage colleagues in understanding its power.
ISBN: 978-04709-45056

TL123   Landmark Issues in Teaching and Learning: A Look Back at New
Directions for Teaching and Learning
Marilla D. Svinicki, Catherine M. Wehlburg
Dr. Marilla Svinicki has been the Editor-in-Chief for *New Directions for
Teaching and Learning* since the early 1990s. As of January 2010, Dr.
Catherine Wehlburg has taken this position. To mark the transition, this
issue focuses on the progress of teaching and learning in higher education
with regard to some important topics that have shaped it during the life of
New Directions for Teaching and Learning. This jointly edited issue is based
on a series of landmark developments in the last thirty years. This issue
provides an overview of where these important topics came from, where
they are presently, and where they are likely to go in the future. Through
this, there is the opportunity to trace the evolution of some of today's most
important developments in teaching and learning.
ISBN: 978-04709-05753

TL122   Pathways to the Profession of Educational Development
Jeanette McDonald, Denise Stockley
Over the last fifty years, educational development has evolved from an informal set of instructional improvement activities championed by individuals
to a scholarly field of study and practice that aims to advance teaching and
learning at the individual, institutional, and (more recently) sector levels.
During this time, educational development work has moved from the fringes
to the mainstream of the higher education landscape, bringing to the community a diverse group of dedicated academic professionals. At the same
time, our scope of practice and the locations and structures in which we
operated have broadened.
The contributors to this volume are academics working directly or indirectly
with teaching and learning centers and professional communities, serving in
the capacity of educational developer, researcher, or specialist; unit manager

or director; or senior administrator. Drawing on survey and interview data, individual experience and perspective, and familiarity with the educational literature, they offer a context to understand and appreciate how the field of educational development, developer practice, and individual pathways have evolved, further highlighting what territory remains to be explored and uncovered.
ISBN: 978-04708-80104

TL121   **Integrated General Education**
Catherine M. Wehlburg
General education has been an essential part of American higher education for a long time. Unfortunately, it is often seen as something to "get out of the way" so that the student can go on to take the more "important" courses within a chosen major. This way of thinking does a disservice to the student, the student's learning, and the overall expectations for a baccalaureate degree. Institutions of higher education have a responsibility to develop a meaningful general education curriculum that cultivates qualities of thinking, communication, and problem solving (to name a few of the general education goals that many institutions share). What is missing from many institutions, though, is the concept of integrating general education with the overall educational curriculum. If this is done, general education courses are no longer something to take quickly so they can be checked off; instead, they become part of the educational development of the student. This integration benefits the student, certainly, but also the larger society—baccalaureate graduates steeped in the liberal arts will become future leaders. Having been prepared with a broad knowledge base, our current students will be able to think more critically and make good use of information to solve problems that have not yet even been identified.
ISBN: 978-04706-26344

TL120   **As the Spirit Moves Us: Embracing Spirituality in the Postsecondary Experience**
Katherine Grace Hendrix, Janice D. Hamlet
During the past decade there has been an increased interest in how members of "first-world" countries cope with growing demands on their time, over-stimulation of the senses, increasing crime rates, and a generally hurried existence. Professors are hardly immune from these forces, and the results cascade onto students, communities, and ultimately, society in general. In contrast to the traditional Western forms of education, which address rational consensus whole eschewing the subjective, a holistic pedagogy suggests that engaging spirituality in one's classroom and profession is necessary for addressing concerns regarding human development and achievement. More specifically, scholars now espouse the value of holistic teaching—teaching that encompasses not only the mind but the soul as well. The contributors in this volume offer diverse vantage points from which to understand the impact of spirituality on well-being, its influence on classroom pedagogy and interpersonal relationships with students and colleagues, and its utility as a coping mechanism. The authors use auto-ethnography to capture the diversity of their perspectives and to display the power of the reflective voice.
ISBN: 978-04705-92632

NEW DIRECTIONS FOR TEACHING AND LEARNING
ORDER FORM SUBSCRIPTION AND SINGLE ISSUES

DISCOUNTED BACK ISSUES:

Use this form to receive 20% off all back issues of *New Directions for Teaching and Learning*.
All single issues priced at **$23.20** (normally $29.00)

TITLE	ISSUE NO.	ISBN

Call 888-378-2537 or see mailing instructions below. When calling, mention the promotional code JBNND
to receive your discount. For a complete list of issues, please visit www.josseybass.com/go/ndtl

SUBSCRIPTIONS: (1 YEAR, 4 ISSUES)

☐ New Order ☐ Renewal

U.S.	☐ Individual: $89	☐ Institutional: $259
CANADA/MEXICO	☐ Individual: $89	☐ Institutional: $299
ALL OTHERS	☐ Individual: $113	☐ Institutional: $333

Call 888-378-2537 or see mailing and pricing instructions below.
Online subscriptions are available at www.onlinelibrary.wiley.com

ORDER TOTALS:

Issue / Subscription Amount: $ _____

Shipping Amount: $ _____
(for single issues only – subscription prices include shipping)

Total Amount: $ _____

SHIPPING CHARGES:
First Item $5.00
Each Add'l Item $3.00

(No sales tax for U.S. subscriptions. Canadian residents, add GST for subscription orders. Individual rate subscriptions must be paid by personal check or credit card. Individual rate subscriptions may not be resold as library copies.)

BILLING & SHIPPING INFORMATION:

☐ **PAYMENT ENCLOSED:** *(U.S. check or money order only. All payments must be in U.S. dollars.)*

☐ **CREDIT CARD:** ☐ VISA ☐ MC ☐ AMEX

Card number _____ Exp. Date _____

Card Holder Name _____ Card Issue # _____

Signature _____ Day Phone _____

☐ **BILL ME:** *(U.S. institutional orders only. Purchase order required.)*

Purchase order # _____
Federal Tax ID 13559302 • GST 89102-8052

Name _____

Address _____

Phone _____ E-mail _____

Copy or detach page and send to: **John Wiley & Sons, PTSC, 5th Floor**
989 Market Street, San Francisco, CA 94103-1741

Order Form can also be faxed to: **888-481-2665**

PROMO JBNND